The Public Pedagogy of
the Master Narrative

Full details of all our publications can be found on http://www.multilingual-matters.com, or by writing to Multilingual Matters, BLOCK, The Fairfax, Pithay Court, Bristol, BS1 3BN, UK.

The Public Pedagogy of the Master Narrative

The Stories We Tell Ourselves about Race and Language Around the World

JPB Gerald

MULTILINGUAL MATTERS
Bristol • Jackson

DOI https://doi.org/10.21832/GERALD9407
Library of Congress Cataloging in Publication Data

Library of Congress Control Number: 2025032231

A catalog record for this book is available from the Library of Congress.
British Library Cataloguing in Publication Data
A catalogue entry for this book is available from the British Library.

ISBN-13: 978-1-80041-940-7 (hbk)
ISBN-13: 978-1-80041-939-1 (pbk)

Multilingual Matters
UK: BLOCK, The Fairfax, Pithay Court, Bristol, BS1 3BN, UK.
USA: Ingram, Jackson, TN, USA.
Authorised Representative: Easy Access System Europe - Mustamäe tee 50, 10621 Tallinn, Estonia, gpsr.requests@easproject.com.

Website: https://www.multilingual-matters.com
Bluesky: @multi-ling-mat.bsky.social
X: Multi_Ling_Mat
Facebook: https://www.facebook.com/multilingualmatters
Blog: https://www.channelviewpublications.wordpress.com

Copyright © 2026 JPB Gerald.

All rights reserved. No part of this work may be reproduced in any form or by any means without permission in writing from the publisher.

The policy of Multilingual Matters/Channel View Publications is to use papers that are natural, renewable and recyclable products, made from wood grown in sustainable forests. In the manufacturing process of our books, and to further support our policy, preference is given to printers that have FSC and PEFC Chain of Custody certification. The FSC and/or PEFC logos will appear on those books where full certification has been granted to the printer concerned.

Typeset by Deanta Global Publishing Services, Chennai, India.

Contents

Prologue	vii
Introduction	1
Book Preview	5
1 A Progressive Paradise?: The Pacific Northwest	14
2 Untruths and Reconciliation: Canada	22
3 It's Time for the Sun to Set: The United Kingdom	30
4 Jim Croc: Australia	39
5 The Purveyors of Public Pedagogy: California	47
6 Trying to 'Nice' It Away: The Midwest	55
7 The 'Right' Kind of Spanish: Mexico	63
8 EFL on a Rampage: South Korea and Japan	71
9 Learning Colonialism: Algeria	79
10 Trapped in the Sunken Place: New England	87
11 The Goodest Country: Finland	95
12 Lacking the Tools: Italy	104
13 Home Sweet Home?: New York City	112
Conclusion	119

Epilogue 131

Acknowledgments 133

Citations! 135

Index 139

Prologue

When I was in the very first semester of my doctoral program in the fall of 2018, I ended my final paper by admitting, probably unwisely, that I wanted to write books, plural, someday. Like many baby academics, I expected I might someday turn my dissertation into a hardcover academic book priced in such a way that few might access it outside of classroom settings, but that's not what happened. A few years later, while the world was shut down, one of my articles caught people's attention, and suddenly I was invited to give (virtual) talks to audiences around the world. After one of my first talks, I was noticed by a publisher – *the same one publishing this book that's in your hands or on your computer* – and, even before I had transitioned from 'doctoral student' to 'doctoral candidate', I had a book deal.

As you all might remember, late 2020/early 2021 was a, let's just say, challenging time, and the challenges have only since increased, especially when it comes to my particular expertise of racism and language education. I had just barely rescued myself from losing my job when I started writing that book, and I was under an immense amount of stress and pressure, especially considering I also had to propose and then write an entire dissertation around the same time. I essentially had no choice but to write as if my hair was on fire, which is a particular challenge given how little hair I have. I sent off the manuscript expecting it to be savaged by reviewers and turned my attention to my studies, only to be surprised in receiving plaudits and praise. It needed to be edited, like all books, but my general vision stayed entirely intact, and it was released to positive reviews. It even got nominated for a prize, which it ultimately lost to one of the scholars I interviewed for this book, but still, for a first effort, one that I hadn't chased but had sort of fallen into my lap, I was proud of what I'd accomplished. But, now what?

Between finishing the manuscript of the first book and securing the deal for this one, a few things happened. First of all, I got diagnosed with ADHD, and while that won't come up too often in this book, it allowed me to feel a lot of relief about things I had long been ashamed of. Second, I graduated, and it was both fun and dispiriting to notice how much more seriously people took what I had to say because my name starts with 'Dr.' now. Third, and at almost exactly the same time, I got a new job, saving myself from bad managers and aligning myself with a team and an organization that seem to value me because of, and not in spite of, The Neurodivergent Way I Do Things, though I've since moved on again to a new opportunity. All of these things combined to give me a considerable and sustainable boost in confidence, and now, when I write, I no longer assume it'll be torn to shreds. I believe in what I'm saying, and I think what I say has value to the field. I also recently wrote another book, a non-academic book for K-12 teachers, which is about neurodivergence and racism, because I can't resist having too many projects to do and also because I needed an outlet to explore that aspect of myself in a way that might help others.

These days, I am not at all a career academic. I was roundly ignored when I submitted applications to tenure-track jobs, and it was for the best, because most of those schools were in extremely homogeneous areas where I wouldn't want my sons to be raised, and you best bet that some of those locations will be covered and criticized in this book. These days, I only bother to engage with academic journals when a friend specifically requests I participate in a special issue they're editing. I still adjunct sometimes, mostly because I enjoy teaching and want to stay connected to future educators, and I loosely maintain a podcast that helps me work out my ideas with scholars, experts and friends. Unlike the first monograph, which emerged from a miasma of fear, stress and flop sweat, I write this book from a very good place, with a more settled career and a niche-but-growing platform through which to spread ideas that are, by and large, taken seriously. If this is the first thing of mine you've ever read, this may all come off conceited, but I assure you, given how rare it is for Black thought and thinkers to be respected, you'd take a moment to be proud, too.

The only problem was, I didn't want to be a one-hit wonder, 'hit' being relative for academia, as it's not like I made anywhere near enough money to quit my day jobs. If the first one was nominated for an award, and the second one didn't expand its scope in some way, it might be seen as a letdown; more honestly, I would have let *myself* down, and I would have been bored. The thing about being a writer with ADHD is I always have to keep not only the audience but myself interested or the whole project will fall apart. With those self-imposed challenges set before me, I had enough motivation to put this prose to paper, and I think I've managed to pull something together that will keep both you and I engaged.

My first book was something of a manifesto about how corroded I felt the English Language Teaching industry is, dependent on hierarchization comprised of, among other things, whiteness and anti-Blackness, capitalism and colonialism. There was interview data included, but it was mostly borne from my brain and my experiences. I couldn't really do that again, because I said what I needed to say and it's up to the industry to either listen or ignore me, and I have a fairly strong suspicion as to which direction they will continue to go. But I made my point.

With all that said, that book was almost exclusively focused on the United States, because that's where I have spent most of my life, with a sprinkling of citations from the UK, Australia, Canada and other places. When I spoke about the book to people who were unfamiliar with my work, I was struck by the revelation that, perhaps because of how narrow the news media is, many people, in both the United States and elsewhere, still think that racism requires the white hoods of the Ku Klux Klan. Moreover, a considerable number of otherwise knowledgeable individuals still think white supremacy impacts education in one very specific and explicit way, especially given recent attempts to thwart and even outlaw Black history, affirmative action, DEI (Diversity, Equity and Inclusion) and the like. Indeed, far too many seem to see whiteness as the stereotypical version descended from the American South. My intent with this work is to provide complexity to the story of contemporary whiteness and racism, to show both that these tentacles stretch far wider than many might assume and also that this system works differently in every context, despite ultimately constructing the same harmful hierarchies through intersecting ideologies of language and ability.

This book still has plenty of sections on the United States, but I pointedly avoided talking about places such as Texas or Mississippi, because I want to focus on all the *other* ways that racism impacts people that might not actually make its way onto your newsfeed. And yes, in every location, language ideologies work hand-in-glove with racial hierarchies, albeit in what I find to be fascinatingly different ways that nonetheless resemble one another. Additionally, the way that people who are racialized as white choose to engage with or avoid engaging with the topic is fairly unique to each context, and you can bet we will be exploring that ubiquitous discomfort.

What you'll find here is an attempt to broaden readers' minds and challenge their assumptions about what racism is and can be. Can racism flourish in a place where almost everyone is white? What about when almost no one is white? Can language education uphold institutional racism even when people of color are the majority of the populace? And is there any hope for us to finally free ourselves from this quagmire?

Centered primarily on interviews with a mix of civilians, practitioners and scholars, this book will chronicle the differences and similarities between the manifestations of white supremacy in 13 different locations and its connections to ideologies of language in each respective context. The book will include brief examinations of race and language in each context – *tied into other axes of oppression, including but not limited to gender, class and ability* – before delving into current issues and the respective experiences and analyses provided by each interviewee, concluding with a final section in which the 13 previous chapters are summarized with solutions for challenging these systemic issues in the classroom, in educational institutions and in society itself.

In short, this will be something of a global tour of the many ways that racism and hierarchies of language hinder honesty and harm society, expanding it beyond its narrow public conception and moving toward possible solutions to challenge its centrality and prominence.

And hopefully I keep you, and me, interested.

Introduction

Bio

I told you a little bit about me up there, and if you've read my other work you can probably skip to the next section, but for everyone else: Hi. My name is J(ustin) P(ierce) B(aldwin) Gerald, I'm a cishet man living on unceded Munsee Lenape territory just north of what most of us know as New York City. I was born and raised in and around Brooklyn and Manhattan, and now I live in Yonkers, which the city really wants you to know is, temporarily, the third largest city in New York State, a strange thing to brag about, but I assure you there are signs everywhere proclaiming this feat.

I'm Black, always have been, and though only diagnosed at 35, have always had ADHD too. I bring that up alongside my racial identity because it has helped me understand my Blackness quite differently even than when I wrote the first draft of my first book, which I finished prior to my ADHD evaluation, though it was published afterwards. Now, although I rarely experienced the intense and stereotypical outbursts of racial slurs many readers might bring to mind when thinking of what racism is, I was in fact treated differently from my white neurodivergent classmates in subtle ways I only truly noticed upon decades-later reflection.

My father is old enough to have experienced said stereotypical outbursts more frequently, and so I really did think that that's what racism 'was'. As I started my career as a language teacher in Daegu, South Korea, I thought it was 'enough' to just be a Black face in a very white profession. I didn't feel the need to discuss the topic beyond my visible identity. But life has a way of making you confront your circumstances, and over time it became clear I needed to speak out if I wanted to have a clear conscience.

I started to consume research – *much of which I'll cite throughout* – on the intersection between race and language, in particular, the work of Nelson Flores, Jonathan Rosa, Ryuko Kubota and Vijay Ramjattan, the latter of whom I now consider a friend. I started having conversations with (white) language educators and academics, many of whom seemed uncomfortable with the discussions, and I thus focused my inquiry on that discomfort. And, as I mentioned above, I started publishing on whiteness and language education, and that's how I ended up in a position to keep opining on the topic up through this very day.

I haven't been a classroom language teacher in many years now, though I do teach language educators when I adjunct, and I keep one foot in the academic space by speaking at conferences – but only when I'm specifically invited. These days, you are likelier to find me in the neurodivergence space that I'm newest to, as I am concerned that the language field is not much interested in changing. I have, however, decided to give it at least one more shove in the right direction, away from harmful language ideologies that uphold racial hierarchization and cause damage to students (and teachers) from racialized backgrounds.

With what work I've done thus far, there should be enough of a trail for people to follow if they want the language education field to be what it promises, but my hope with this book is to show that racism is vast and confusing, and that no one country – *not even the United States* – has a monopoly on the concept.

Some Key Terms and Concepts

At the risk of seeming lethargic, I have used many of these terms before, and my interest is in comparing the impact within different contexts. So, this part is heavily based upon my prior work (for the same publisher), and if JPB Gerald wants to sue me, he can go right ahead.

So, *racism* is the combination of racial discrimination and societal oppression. Anyone can experience the former, but only certain people can experience the mixture and the compounded impact thereof. For example, as a Black person, I could tell you I don't want to date a white person – *this is just for the sake of argument* – and that would absolutely be discrimination, but because I do not have the full power of society behind me, and because that would not materially impact the people I denied my attention, it does not qualify. It's just not a nice thing to do, and racism is a system of power and hierarchy rather than interpersonal cruelty. An important point to add here is that race is, of course, not biological fact; nothing happens to people because of their race but because of the system of *racism* – to be Biblical for a moment, racism begets race. The reason I'm nervous when I'm pulled over by the police is racism, not my race.

Additionally, it is important that when we speak of harm being visited upon Black people specifically – *which won't factor into every chapter of this book, but will on occasion* – we know that we are speaking of *anti-Blackness*. Anti-Blackness is oppression of Black people, Black bodies, Black languages and Black languaging. It is another way of saying *anti-Black racism*, one of many forms of racism, also including anti-Asian racism, but not anti-white racism or reverse racism, despite what some folks will try to tell you. I point this out because people often ask what it's called when, say, an Asian person helps to oppress a Black person, and that's why anti-Blackness is a useful term. You will certainly hear about this phenomenon in certain sections of this book.

As I have said many times in my writing career, there is no real difference between whiteness and white supremacy. Indeed, whiteness, as a concept, was created to justify colonialism and chattel slavery (Painter, 2011); there had to be a group that could never be targeted by this system, and as such, whiteness came to exist as a protection from the worst of our societies.

We cannot speak of racism and whiteness without discussing *colonialism*, and in particular the *settler colonialism* visited upon the indigenous and the enslaved peoples of what was eventually named the United States. As Dunbar-Ortiz (2014: 2) explained, this system represented 'the founding of a state based on the ideology of white supremacy, the widespread practice of African slavery, and a policy of genocide and land theft'. Colonialism is, of course, not at all an American invention, and this is part of the reason for my writing this book – we not only didn't invent it, but in some ways we are farther removed from the system than other places we'll discuss in later chapters.

Language ideologies descend from – and help uphold – broadly shared societal views about languages and the people who use them, and have a massive influence on communication and standardization in a given context (Ricento, 2013). These ideologies govern language policy and planning, for the ostensibly unbiased goals of pragmatism and economic development. American identity, for example, is tied to the usage of English. 'A principal means of achieving Americanization was through massive education programs that sought to teach American values, ways of thinking, ways of living, and especially the national language, English' (Ricento, 2013: 4). Additionally, language ideologies create the parameters of a supposed 'standard' language, which is then viewed more highly than other languages and against which people are compared. 'Persons speaking other stigmatized ("nonstandard") varieties tend to be viewed as having deficiencies in intelligence, morality, and/or character and are often less successful in achieving upward social mobility, which generally requires proficiency in the standard "national" language' (Ricento, 2013: 5).

Finally, though this book is not centered on economic systems, we must touch on capitalism, or, as Cedric Robinson describes it, *racial capitalism*. Robinson (1983: 3) explained in his treatise on the concept: 'The development, organization, and expansion of capitalist society pursued essentially racial directions, so too did social ideology.' Robinson (1983: 4) does not argue that thinkers such as Marx and Engels were wrong so much as that their 'theory of revolution was insufficient in scope'.

Quite importantly for some of the contexts in which this book will operate is a linguistic construction you might have already noticed, words such as *minoritized, racialized* and *standardized*. In all such instances, these words are an attempt to push back on decisions made by dominant groups. Minoritized, for example, is a more accurate way to describe the Black citizens of Detroit, Michigan or South Africa, where, in each case, they comprise the numerical majority but have long held far less power than the white numerical minority – they have been forcibly placed in the minority position. Similarly, racialized indicates that race is not an incontrovertible biological fact but a classification that is context dependent and has evolved over time (Omi & Winant, 2014); for example, the word 'Asian' refers to different groups in the United States and the United Kingdom, a place to which we will certainly travel before this book ends.

Okay. I have finished re-hashing previous definitions and updating them for this work. It's time to preview the argument and the story I intend to tell here, and provide a justification for your continued attention.

Book Preview

This book has 13 chapters, followed by a conclusion reflecting on all that's been learned about racism, white supremacy and language ideologies from the findings in all the previous pages. Each chapter will be structured more or less the same way, with some information about its racial demographics, perceptions of race and language, followed by the reality, as shared by contemporary scholarship, news stories, popular culture and the interviews I conducted. I was clear that I didn't only want the opinions of academics, as we academics can often live in fantasy worlds of intellectual ephemera, but there are still plenty of us across these pages, for better or worse. With that said, I also spoke to people I knew with what I thought would be interesting insight into the context. When appropriate I will include my own thoughts on the location, if I've spent any time there, as my status as a Black person always causes interesting reactions when I travel, but mostly I will leave it to the research to speak to the concepts as much as possible.

The following are the places I've chosen and the reasons for doing so.

1. The Pacific Northwest

In this case, I am referring mostly to what most know of as Oregon and Washington State, though as with many of the places I've chosen, I selected the Pacific Northwest (PNW) area because of my own perception of the place's public perception – *yes, a perception of a perception* – and I wanted to start there because of its general reputation as a progressive area with strong values. Think of the multicultural nature of Seattle, the left-leaning stereotypes you often see coming out of Portland (or the TV show *Portlandia*). These values would suggest a lack of racism, but I also already knew that there are deeply ugly events in the region's past – *and present* – that those with only a passing familiarity with the area would be unaware of and surprised to learn about. But, I've only ever been out there twice, and while I will share what my experience was like, I am not well-versed in the culture, so hopefully this chapter will further enlighten me as well as readers.

The chapter will also seek to answer the following question: How do language ideologies and practices uphold racial hierarchies – *and vice versa* – in this context, and how do English and other colonial languages reify these harmful systems? *(This being the primary research question of the book, it will be addressed in every chapter, so I won't repeat it 12 more times in this preview.)*

2. Canada

Similarly to my reasons for choosing the Pacific Northwest, Canada is often framed as the 'nicer' northern neighbor to the United States. However, though bolstered by its own government and popular culture, this reputation masks a bloody colonial history, as is true of any part of the supposed 'Commonwealth of Nations'. I do not seek to rub readers' faces in trauma and violence, and, although I'll bring it up as it is necessary to make my point, I want to focus less on What Canada Did (and Does) but more on how shocked its (white) citizens seem to be whenever another atrocity is quite literally uncovered. As with some of the chapters on regions of the United States, Indigeneity and its relationship to whiteness and language will factor into the discussion.

Now, Canada is obviously a massive country (to have stolen), so I do not claim to have exhaustively catalogued how whiteness and language operate in every disparate region; this is true of other chapters as well. Indeed, this is more about the way people perceive Canada's racism in comparison to the, for lack of a better word, Racism Classic (™) that emanated from the Jim Crow South.

3. The United Kingdom

Speaking of the Commonwealth, the crown itself was probably the direct inspiration for this book and its approach. I speak with scholars and citizens of the UK quite often, and hearing how my own work on race, whiteness and language has been viewed there – *a wide range between vitriol and celebration* – has been one of the more fascinating parts of my relatively brief career as an author. Indeed, some of my biggest champions – *including this publisher* – are British, while some of the nastiest racist comments I've received were from the same small island. I even had a British educator essentially follow me around the internet for years, writing blog posts about me and my work every chance he got, even going so far as to create fake social media accounts after I blocked him, until he abruptly stopped one day, which was weird.

Since this book is about English, it would be silly if I didn't devote a chapter to the country that started all of this, and I can probably bet you that if there's a particular chapter in which to expect the level of viciousness you may remember from my first book, it's this one, because so many language ideologies and colonialist practices are, in one way or another, extremely British. Simply put, the UK represents the epitome of what I am trying to explore in this book – a place that, from all evidence I can find, is no less racist than my country but considers itself distant from the behavior in which we engage. But maybe my expectations will prove to have been challenged when I dig into the research and the interviews. We will see.

4. Australia

I think that people who know very little about Australia might consider the country fun and peaceful. Frankly, I knew very little about it myself and it might have been what I assumed if I were to have planned a trip down there while I was living in Asia, although I got pretty close when I went to Bali. So this chapter is one of the ones I was most interested in writing, because I learned a lot of fairly shocking things that I truly never had the slightest clue about. Sure, in some ways, there are similarities to the other Commonwealth countries on this list, but it's distant enough that it really does have its own flavor of racism. I probably shouldn't have been as surprised as I was – *it's a Commonwealth country after all* – but I really was floored by what I learned, and maybe you will be too. And, as ever, the racial hierarchies cannot be divorced from language ideologies.

5. California

Back to the States for a few chapters now.

California is seen as a progressive state, albeit a much more diverse one than the Pacific Northwest states I mentioned earlier. It's well-known that many Californians speak languages other than English, and there have been court cases about legal battles over English.

But California is also a big state, both in size and, especially, in population. There are more people in California than there are in all of Australia or Canada. When you have that many people and cultures, you are bound to have conflict – *we will get to homogenous places later and the way racism festers there* – and there's a lot to dig into when it comes to race and language in this state that is responsible for a significant portion of the world's popular culture. A lot of what we – *and by 'we', I mean Americans, English users and, frankly, humans* – both learn and propagate about race comes out of California, so examining this location ought to be illuminating for the analysis I'm attempting.

What I expect you'll find here is a state that preaches progressive values but also has firm hierarchies that seem to contradict its ideals. Read on to said chapter to gain additional insight into how that manifests.

6. The Midwest

For the unfamiliar, the Midwest – *so named because the country started in the East and it's sort of 'midway' to the West Coast* – is a broad, amorphous area that, depending on who you're talking to, starts in Western New York State and Pennsylvania, extends to Minnesota and down to parts of Missouri. Some classify it differently, and limit it to the states that border the Great Lakes. But it's a massive section of the United States, and it always seems to determine who is in the White House every four years.

It's also well known for being friendly and chipper, with the phrase 'Minnesota Nice' a common refrain. If you've ever seen the Coen brothers' movie *Fargo – which doesn't actually take place in Fargo, North Dakota, but rather Minnesota –* think of the movie's heroine, police officer Marge Gunderson, who, even in the face of greed and brutality, maintains her upbeat nature and saves the day, or whatever of the day is left to be saved after the events of the movie. Go watch it if you haven't, it's a classic.

But there's another side to the history of the Midwest, and, you've read far enough to predict what I'm going to say, but there's a very specific reason I've chosen the region, and it starts with Dr. James Loewen. Dr. Loewen, who passed away of cancer in 2021, was a white historian who dedicated his career to challenging America's founding myths. The first book of his I read was *Lies My Teacher Told Me: Everything Your American History Textbook Got Wrong* (1995), which is exactly what its title portends, and indeed taught me more about true American history than I ever learned in school. It was another one of his books, though, that had a greater influence on my own career.

A decade after *Lies My Teacher Told Me*, Loewen published *Sundown Towns: A Hidden Dimension of American Racism* (2005). Now, the concept of a 'sundown town' – *so named because, for the purpose of commerce, Black people were allowed to work in the towns but had to leave by dusk under pain of death, and therefore could not actually live there* – was not actually 'hidden' to Black people. I knew about them from what my father had told me about his childhood, even if he used different terminology. But what made the book so impactful for me was that Loewen was inspired to do said research – *research that continues even after his death –* because he found out that *his* hometown was once a sundown town, and his hometown was not in the South but in the Midwest (in the state of Illinois, to be specific). For a white scholar to basically dedicate his career to uncovering the ugliness from which he himself emerged was an act of honesty, and convinced me of something I believe to this day: that white readers of this book or another are fully capable of the work it takes to divest themselves from the white supremacist ideals all around them. I even wrote my dissertation about white educators trying to do such a thing, and most of the people I interviewed were, in fact, located in the Midwest.

So the Midwest is a fascinating dichotomy, a smile plastered atop of rage and blood. And I hope to share with you some insights I've gleaned from how they have – *and mostly haven't* – grappled with their truth in the same way that Dr. Loewen did.

7. Mexico

Mexico sits in an interesting place culturally, as well as geographically. They are obviously greatly influenced by whatever nonsense we get up to in the States, while also being neighbors with countries under tremendous strain. They end up, accordingly, at the literal center of extremely racist anti-immigration policies, as many of the people who enter the United States via Mexico are not from Mexico at all.

But while Mexico is in some ways oppressed, that by no means absolves the country of its own hierarchization, which is, yes, often based on racial categories and language. The Indigenous populations of Mexico have suffered in ways quite similar to those of the United States and Canada, and, at the same time, these are the individuals least likely to have a chance to be treated as 'white', even if it's thought of somewhat differently. I'll provide more detail and citations in the chapter, but suffice it to say that the stratification in Mexico not being as different from that of the United States as you might expect shouldn't be that surprising considering that, like English in the United States, there's a pretty clear settler colonial reason they speak Spanish in the first place.

8. South Korea and Japan

The choice to combine the two in this chapter may yet get me yelled at by the combined populations of both, but hear me out.

In no way will I be arguing that the two countries and cultures are the same. There's only one of the two that spent World War II trying to cosplay as Germany East. But, in more recent years, the way that the English as a Foreign Language industry has infiltrated both places is actually somewhat similar. Point being, I do think that the interaction between whiteness and language education can be effectively compared, and used as an example of what happens when a region that truly has very few white bodies imports thousands thereof as baubles for the sake of commerce. I've written about my years in South Korea many times over by now, so I won't rehash it too much in this chapter, but the fact that I could go from a fully unemployed college graduate to a teacher entrusted with several hundred students in a few weeks continues to be a cause for concern. So how can the industry have planted itself so firmly in both countries, and what can we possibly do about it?

9. Algeria

Speaking of the continent of Africa, most people from Algeria are seen as quite distinct from people from Nigeria or Zambia both geographically and culturally. North Africa is usually lumped in with the Middle East when ethnic groups are unofficially categorized in the United States, forming what is referred to as the 'MENA' (Middle East North Africa) population. There are understandable reasons for this given the basic fact of the Sahara desert and the often-different religions and customs, but on top of this, the proximity to Europe creates an in-between position that allows for a different reality when it comes to race and language.

Indeed, given the distribution of the population centers (and that same desert), when you're talking about Algerians, you are often really talking about the Mediterranean coast itself, so to take a look at the way Europe's behavior has shaped what is essentially an oppressed neighbor ought to provide valuable insight into the discussion this book intends to put forward.

10. New England

Back over to the United States, I want to talk about New England because it's an interesting mirror image of the Pacific Northwest in some ways. For the unaware, New England is essentially the corner of the United States that starts once you leave the New York City metropolitan area and continues up until you reach the Canadian border. Given that my wife and her family are from Connecticut, I spend a lot of time there, and, again like the Pacific Northwest, it is an interesting mix of progressive values and politicians alongside a rather striking homogeneity.

When I was thinking about where to work after I finished my doctorate, a lot of schools in New England were hiring for jobs in what I considered to be my disciplines, but when I looked at the towns where the schools were located, I was flabbergasted at just how white they were, upward of 90% in some cases. I wasn't comfortable raising my (at the time only) son in such an environment, yet New England has a reputation for being pro-civil rights and diversity that it *sort of* deserves.

New England, as its name suggests, was the place the original colonists used to start the country I now live in. Our nominal values descend from this area. The war that allowed us to become a country was fought almost entirely within this region. It is extremely proud of itself.

But I'm not so sure it should be.

11. Finland

Did you know that Finns, at one point, weren't even considered white in the United States? It's true. I'm sure you've heard that about the Irish and the Italians – *maybe even in my first book* – but it's true of Finland as well.

The reasons for this particular instance of conditional whiteness are complex, but I include Finland here because of its slightly less prominent placement when compared to Norway and Sweden. It's farther east, it's colder and it's not quite as wealthy. Accordingly, they get treated differently.

I wanted to speak about at least one Nordic country because of a particular book I read once, which I'll cite when I get to this chapter. In this book, the Finnish system of education is made out to be not just superior to the United States but nearly flawless. I am not disputing its potential superiority, but I do want to trouble its perception as relatively free from the hierarchies that we are often (rightly) accused of perpetuating. Essentially, I want to trouble the Nordic apotheosis.

12. Italy

Speaking of people once not seen as white, I wanted to explore a bit of how these ideas are filtered through an analysis of immigration. Italy is sort of on the flipside of Algeria, a short jaunt across the sea from Northern Africa. They occupy an interesting space in the United States, often serving as police officers for historical reasons I'll explore, yet within their own country, race and language are seen differently from what you might otherwise expect. But in other ways, they are more similar to the United States than one might have assumed, with a stark difference between the North and South. This chapter will certainly be tied to the previous ones on the United States, but it will be interesting to consider how they have and haven't changed since they were added to the conditional category of 'white'.

13. New York City

And finally, my home town, where I actually no longer live, though I'm only a few miles north. Like a lot of the places I've mentioned, it's considered a progressive and diverse place, and it's certainly the latter, but I've watched as we've treated immigrants terribly, created policies with direct racist impact and acted as though we were above this sort of behavior. People from outside of the city think of it as far more dangerous than it is, but even people who live there harbor unfortunate raciolinguistic fears that have a tangible impact on its citizens. Ultimately, the imaginary terror they feel only harms the most vulnerable people in the city. I will share with you the love I have for the place, the actions the city has taken that woke me up to the racism and language hierarchization around me, and the reasons I finally gave up and left. As a hint, it wasn't because of the supposed dangers, but the people who believed in and perpetuated the idea that the dangers existed.

Okay. But, Really. Why *These* People and Places?

I will be honest and say that pragmatism factored into a lot of how I sourced the people I interviewed. Originally this book was going to be called ***Fifteen** Shades of White*, because I think I'm funny, but then it changed to Thirteen *Shades of White* because I couldn't find people to interview in two of the locations which, for the record, were Florida and South Africa. I don't mean I didn't have people in mind so much as that they, as academics, were too busy to sit for interviews, because academics be like that. And then, after all that, the publisher said *Thirteen Shades of White* didn't work as a title – *because now the pun doesn't work* – so I came up with this one, which is no longer a pun, and that makes me sad. Anyway, our inability to connect ties into my reasoning for selecting these people – as you'll find throughout the book, I am often very frustrated with the structures of academia, which is the main reason why that is not my primary career. Accordingly, the answer to your – *and one of the initial reviewers'* – question is simply, the individuals you'll hear from were willing and able to speak to me.

Now, there is also the added factor that almost all of them are academics or educators of some sort. But to be completely honest, I don't get along with most academics, because we aren't trained to speak to the public effectively and I believe that renders us less relevant than we ought to be. Accordingly, although I did want to find people who had the training to both conduct and understand research but also the personality that made them inclined to mostly avoid jargon and be direct with me, even if behind pseudonyms. Many of them are also white, which is, yes, for convenience given who I know professionally, yet is also intentional in that I wanted to hear how white residents of certain areas behaved, and people who look like me are never going to receive that level of honesty from our white peers. Additionally, it would be silly of me to pretend that I didn't anticipate that most people reading this are probably also white, and as such there is an implied challenge to you, that if the people interviewed could grapple with these concepts directly, then you ought to be able to do so as well. Sure, the truly comprehensive method would have been to travel to each place and speak to ordinary citizens, and if you would like to fund that work, I will be accepting donations on my website.

The fact of the matter is, this is by no means a work that attempts to be all-encompassing, but rather a narrative about narratives from the perspectives of your author here and the community he was and is connected to. We may well be 'wrong', but we are most assuredly less incorrect than the stories we've all been told, and have told ourselves. I hope that you will accept and engage with our story and its attempts to change the master narrative, a phrase I will soon define in detail, before you ask.

Ultimately, the question you have to ask yourself is this – are you more willing to accept a story you've been told your entire life by powerful people invested in holding onto their status, or a series of stories told by, admittedly, a bunch of nerds who would like to challenge that orthodoxy? This book makes many references to movies, which, depending on your belief in the concept of auteurs, are often the stories crafted by just one person, or a few people. This work is nominally non-fiction, but, if it helps, consider this a movie that hopes to revise a part of race and language history. I hope that it's both informative and entertaining the whole way through.

And so, there you have it. Thirteen places. Cities, states, regions, countries, sometimes more than one country at once. Some of the chapters cover a few million people, some cover 20 million, some cover nearly 200 million. The people interviewed are not meant to represent an entire location or identity, but were people I thought could help provide compelling shading to a new narrative around race and language in their particular context. But I assure you that I learned a great deal about whiteness and language through my interviews and other research, and I expect you'll learn a lot as well. Whiteness isn't just what you see on the news, or what you read on social media; despite its name, it is not monochromatic. So let's begin our journey around the world and learn to recognize these 13 shades of white. (Look, I still had to make the joke ONCE.)

1 A Progressive Paradise?

The Pacific Northwest

Here's how these chapters are mostly going to be laid out: we will start with a fairly rote description of the racial and linguistic demographics and metrics of the selected region(s). We can call that portion of each chapter **Background**. Then, I will explore the way that, from my own perspective and experience, racial hierarchies are generally perceived. We will call that portion **Perception**. Then, using the interviews I conducted and other current data, we will try to ground ourselves in the truth. We can call that portion **Reality**. And finally, we will reflect on what we've learned in portions we will call **What Needs to Happen**. And then sometimes I'll do things differently to keep you on your toes.

Background

What we call the states of Washington and Oregon is, like the rest of the country, stolen from Indigenous populations, in this case a wide array of peoples including names since repurposed into cities that are mostly white, including Sauk Suiattle and Walla Walla, along with other tribes such as the still-prominent Squamish Nation, though their presence is felt more keenly north of the (imaginary) border in British Columbia, Canada.

There are approximately 8 million people in Washington State, about 70% of whom are white, with no other racial category comprising more than 10% of the population (World Population Review, 2023). So, unlike some other states or regions we will speak about in later chapters, it's not so much that it's a racially homogenous state but more that all other racial groups are somewhat poorly represented – that remaining 30% is spread fairly evenly across many groups. I can attest to believing in the statistic that the state is only 3% Black – I didn't see a single face similar to mine last time I visited Seattle, aside from others attending the TESOL Conference at which I was presenting.

As for Oregon, it is significantly larger than Washington – *it is the 9th largest state, while Washington is 18th* – but much more sparsely populated, especially outside of its northwest corner (where Portland is located). There are just over 4 million people in the state, and it is significantly whiter than Washington, at nearly 79% (World Population Review, 2023). In both states, the racial group in second place is 'Asian', which in this case refers to East and Southeast Asia, as Pacific Islanders are combined with Native Hawaiians. In Oregon, the Asian population is only 4% of the state. So, yeah, it's not very diverse. In addition, there is a disquietingly large trend of violent, far-right Christian Nationalism that has taken hold in the more rural parts of both states (Center for Democratic Renewal, n.d.). If you have ever seen the movie *Green Room – in which a struggling rock band takes a gig and comes to realize, far too late, that they're playing for Neo-Nazis, and then a lot of people die* – it was filmed, and takes place, in Oregon. No, not *Green* Book. You don't need to see that.

In the introduction, I mentioned the concept of 'sundown towns', but in the case of Oregon, what we have is a former sundown *state*. According to the Oregon Remembrance Project (2023), 'When Oregon became a state in 1859, it entered into the Union with Black exclusionary laws, essentially making it a "whites only state." In 1890, 17 of Oregon's 32 counties had 0–10 African Americans living in them. However, by 1930, 28 of Oregon's 32 counties had 0–10 African Americans living in them. African Americans were pushed from rural communities into condensed urban settings. It is estimated that most of Oregon was once a sundown town.' Lovely.

Accordingly, you can trace the homogenous population of the current state to the way it was founded, and keep in mind this was after stealing the land in the first place. I would argue that it is simply never an accident when an American state is that white – if we Black folks thought it was a place we should be, we would have moved there during the Great Migration. There are plenty of us in California after all (though we'll get to Californian racism in that chapter). So this is the context, both anodyne and ugly, from which the Pacific Northwest generates its reputation.

Perception

With all of that said about violence and exclusion, that is not the image the region projects, nor one I knew anything about before my doctoral studies exposed me to said history. When I thought of these states, I suppose I thought of tech giants such as Microsoft and Amazon being located in the Seattle area, the origin of Starbucks coffee, and, you know, rain. As for Oregon, my perceptions were influenced by everything I heard about leftist organizing in and around Portland, and a general loving vibe. I also assumed that there was more effective integration of both immigrant and Indigenous cultures, and while that does exist, as we just learned, the states are overwhelmingly white – by comparison, according to the Census, the United States is a little less than 60% white, and that percentage is gradually declining (US Dept of Commerce, 2024).

If you're a bit younger than I am – *39 as I make my final edits, older by the time you read them* – you might associate the area with the

Twilight film series, which was in fact filmed in and around Washington, and accurately conveys its beauty. As a brief note here, films and other popular culture have already been mentioned several times and will continue to be because they are a curriculum we all consume collectively, one that absolutely shapes our perceptions, including of race and language. Accordingly, while me or you might eagerly go online to consume the contents of a research journal, most people do not have access to these sources, and would understandably find them dull and disengaging. So, in bringing up *Twilight*, I am not endorsing the movie series, which is silly, but pointing out that it is both a product of and a creator of peoples' perceptions of the Pacific Northwest, except I hope people don't really believe the Indigenous population turns into wolves. I joke, but that series does bring me back to my assumption of greater diversity than there actually is in the region.

There's a story that exemplifies both my former assumptions as well as highlighting what is hiding under the surface. In the summer of 2020, when a great many white citizens were participating in their brief moment of empathy for Black lives, I heard about the so-called 'Wall of Moms' and the heroic work they were doing. According to Zoellner (2020),

> Enraged by previous nights of violent altercations between officers and demonstrators, the 'Wall of Moms' group formed with up to 100 mothers linking arms in front of the federal courthouse starting from Saturday evening. Their goal? To stand as a wall between federal officers deployed by the Trump administration and demonstrators who were there to protest racial injustice and police brutality across the country.

Great. This confirmed what I'd long believed about the Pacific Northwest, that it was a place that, even if it turns out it was more homogenous than I'd assumed, the white citizens were more eager to stand up for someone like me than anywhere else in the country. From later in the same piece, 'One reason behind [a Black woman named in the article] working behind the scenes of the protests instead of standing on the front lines was because the white women in the group wanted to use their race as a barrier to protect women of colour.' Fantastic! But then what happened?

That original story was posted on July 24, 2020. By August 3 – all of *10 days later* – the organization had essentially splintered due to controversy, mismanagement and, most relevantly for this work, anti-Black racism. As Blaec (2020) writes,

> There was a reckoning over Zoom on July 29, with speculation running rampant that Barnum had big plans to commodify and monetize this movement while insisting that Black Lives Matter was only ever 'a piece'

of the Wall of Moms. Facebook fights and phone calls riddled with anti-Blackness and misogynoir ensued, leading to contradicting takes on what exactly led the group to dissolve.

For the unfamiliar, *misogynoir* is the particular sort of combined racism and sexism experienced by Black women specifically. But the point is, the leader saw the movement grow in prominence and decided to try to cash in on it, which was not, everyone else believed, the point. This was followed by racist social media commentary and just as soon as it had been created and reached international news, the Wall of Moms was shattered. This is just one happening, yes, but my own scholarly career was starting around this time, with my second-ever article (Gerald, 2020), about whiteness and language teaching, being published in May of that year, and I was paying very close attention to stories like this. The Wall of Moms helped me understand how supposed allyship could be punctured in such a short period of time, and is why I wanted to start this book by talking about Washington and Oregon.

The moral of the story is, whereas I, like many people, once believed Washington and Oregon were warm, progressive places where I'd feel safe and welcomed if I were to ever move there – *like my best friend did, though he's white* – it turns out that, before conducting these interviews and delving into the extant research, it wasn't so much a racial utopia but more of a place that would like people to *think* is a racial utopia, a place where white suburban moms go viral for protecting Black lives while disparaging and diminishing them behind the scenes. Stories like the Wall of Moms are mere anecdotes, sure, but we are speaking of perception here, and such perceptions help to create the master narrative under which we all live. And yes, now you get your definition of a phrase that's on the book's cover: The *master narrative*, according to Hammack and Toolis (2015), is a dominant cultural script that shapes our beliefs and behaviors, and indeed much of what I write about in these Perception portions will be my own interaction with the master narrative of a given place. And, as you might expect given its name, a master narrative seeks to control what we think, and in doing this work, I am hoping to upend these stories we've all been told, or at least to provide some additional, as the title of the book says, shading.

Reality

'So the Pacific Northwest, from my perspective', Dr. Mary Birch (*all names are pseudonyms unless otherwise indicated*) told me.

> It fits in with a lot of stereotypes about 'wokeness,' right? So people talk about race and racism in this very sort of studied way where it's like there are the right things to say about it and the wrong things to say about it. And like we're the good kind of white people who like everyone, you

know, and it's interesting to me because it's such a white place, and it still puts such an emphasis on being welcoming when the experience of Black people I know has not been feeling welcomed.

Dr. Birch is a (white) language scholar who has recently relocated to the Midwest – *so you'll hear from her again in that chapter* – after spending the last several years working at a university in Oregon. She's someone I trust to be honest and direct with me on these things in a way that the Pacific Northwest would probably rather her not be, and you can mentally append that description to everyone subsequently interviewed so I don't have to repeat it dozens of times.

'If I tell my friends in the Pacific Northwest about [son's name]'s daycare', she continued, 'they're like, "Oh, it's wonderful that he's exposed to diversity," where diversity is just code for like, he's exposed to Black people as if that's some sort of prize for him.'

That final sentence there is important. White American parents often split into two camps, those who see additional diversity as a bauble – *either for their kids or their own pride* – or they object to 'wokeness' and find the entire concept offensive (Himmelstein, 2021). When it comes to the Pacific Northwest, then, her assessment of the context matched the image of what the area has tried to put forth.

Hannah, a K-12 English Language teacher from the Seattle area, told me how much of a contrast she noticed when she traveled to other cities that were legitimately diverse. 'When I went to Philadelphia', she explained, 'It's embarrassing to say it was 2019 and I went and I said, "Oh, this is diversity." I don't live in a diverse place like that. I don't. And it's embarrassing that it was that late, to be 2019 for me to notice that but I knew I knew it wasn't diverse to begin with.'

'In high school', she continued, 'in my high school yearbook, my senior year, the one kid who was very dark-skinned, he was blue in the yearbook in his senior photo because all the pictures were white kids. So they didn't have the photography skills or whatever they were doing with the pictures that that photo turned out that way.'

When taking this discussion over to linguistic ideologies, both concurred that views on languages and languaging are used as a means of expressing racism in a more acceptable way. 'People don't want to say the wrong thing', Hannah said. 'But you can talk about people who don't have the "right" language skills. And you might be saying something that's factually true depending on what we're using. And therefore, you can get away with saying something about different racial groups.'

'There's all this discourse', she said, 'about people who, when they migrate here, where they grew up here, who don't speak English a certain way, like the sort of connection between which language they speak and the way you speak on intelligence you know, it's just really acceptable to denigrate the language right. And I would point out that that could be construed as racist.'

Her reference to 'the way you speak on intelligence' is because I've written and spoken about how peoples' language skills are often seen as a proxy for their intelligence. If someone cannot communicate in an acceptable way, their ideas need not be taken as seriously, a process that has been going on since – *at least* – the colonial era, when the members of enslaved or indigenous groups that could approximate the language of the conquerors were seen as more civilized (Mills & Lefrancois, 2018). Fanon (1952) put it more eloquently than I ever could:

> Every colonized people – in other words, every people in whose soul an inferiority complex has been created by the death and burial of its local cultural originality – finds itself face to face with the language of the civilizing nation; that is, with the culture of the mother country. The colonized is elevated above his jungle status in proportion to his adoption of the mother country's cultural standards. (Fanon, 1952: 18)

'When I teach my language and power class', Dr. Birch told me, 'that's the primary lesson that I want students to recognize. Like, language is the last acceptable vestige of prejudice, right? People can say all sorts of absolutely inappropriate things about somebody's language that they would never say about them just based on their race, but they'd say, "well, they speak in a really sloppy way." Well, sloppy is so coded or even saying, and I'm sure you have personally experienced this, people talking about somebody being "articulate." That's not nice. *Maybe* they mean it in a nice way. But what they're saying is, for a Black person, you sound white. That's what they're saying. Right?'

Right.

'In order for us to live in a society that I think a lot of the progressive folks, especially in the Pacific Northwest, want to live in', Dr. Birch said, 'they have to cede so much of their power and they're not willing to see that power, right. And they're not willing to see that privilege and what they want is for everybody to have the same amount of privilege and the same amount of power. But I think what isn't really realized is, that's going to require you to give something up. Are you willing to give up real tangible power in your life? And I don't think many white people are willing to do that.'

And of course, when the environment is historically hostile enough to scare many people of color away from even establishing roots in a region, then who is going to be positioned to challenge said power imbalance?

Hannah confirmed this analysis by relating the way that her white colleagues used linguistic ideologies and coded language to combine classism and racism.

Title One is code for the schools that have more kids of color. And in that building, it was mostly white teachers. And they would say things like, 'if you can survive teaching here, you could teach anywhere, because you're at this school'. Because of where my district is, because most of the district is upper middle class or upper class because of the property values and stuff. Like my school was situated in a low income neighborhood, so it was like, 'Oh, the Title One school' or 'Oh, you get the national board bonus at your school.' So like you said they use these different coded ways to talk about it. And the teaching staff is very, very white in a lot of places, very white and female. But it is coded because you wouldn't say 'oh, that first school with a lot of Hispanic kids,' you'd say, 'oh, it's the Title One school, it's the high poverty school.' And, 'Oh, those kids, that's a hard school to be at,' those kinds of things come out with that.

A few notes here for international readers:

- American school districts are often funded by property taxes (i.e. taxes on homes and similar structures), so the more affluent districts tend to have better-funded schools. Many parents will scheme to 'get into' a better district, by which they mean find a way to move there prior to school enrollment.
- 'Title One' and the 'National Boards Bonus' refer to the Title I federal policy that provides extra funding to schools with a high percentage of socioeconomically disadvantaged students, which is another way of saying 'poor'.
- The American teacher population is overwhelmingly both white and female (Will, 2020).

What Needs to Happen

From Dr. Birch:

I was shocked when I moved to the Pacific Northwest because I didn't know all of the history. Like I guess I knew there was a racist past to Oregon but I didn't realize how recent that racist past really was. You know, there's a reason why Eugene doesn't really have any Black people living in it and the same thing is true for Portland. But I think you don't have to make the hard decisions at all right? Because you can like, sit comfortably in your wokeness and say all the right things without ever having to live the consequences of saying those right things.

If I am to trust her assessment, then what needs to change is a combination of things that might be challenging and unlikely. I would say that more of the area's history needs to be revealed and promoted to those who are raised there, but, all of this information is easily searchable across the internet, and, as is usually the case, the people of color don't need to be taught what's already happened to them. We are in a bit of a Catch-22 situation here: there aren't enough residents of color, so there isn't enough pressure on the dominant population to educate themselves – *and the educators themselves are white* – on what they've long engaged in. And why would anyone who wouldn't feel safe as part of the environment choose to become a part of it?

There is good work being done by those who care enough to do it. You can say we need to teach this to schoolchildren, and we should, but those schools are run by adults, and those adults are going to have to be vulnerable enough to engage in the sort of reflection Dr. Birch and Hannah described above. Are the people of the Pacific Northwest willing to look directly at themselves and take note of the hierarchies they've perpetuated in a way that goes beyond subsuming racist ideologies under linguistic ones? Or, as I suspect, will it continue to be a place that is able to cocoon itself in a misleading image? As noted above, even Dr. Birch, who studies these sorts of things, was caught off guard by the reality upon arrival, and she didn't suggest to me she thought things had improved in any way upon her departure. We'll return to Dr. Birch later, as she has only moved to a different region in full denial of its complicity, but for now, we will travel slightly north to a place that many of us think is very, very friendly.

2 Untruths and Reconciliation

Canada

Background

One of my favorite things to do as a geography nerd – *look, I'm a lot of different kinds of nerd* – is to compare seemingly disparate things to see how similar they actually are. For example, as I learned in French class in junior high school, 'La France est la taille de Texas' – France is the size of Texas. Now, that's not actually accurate – *France is about 80% the size of Texas* (My Life Elsewhere, n.d.) – but it's the sort of fact that gets me thinking about how our perceptions are warped by factors such as Texas merely being one of 50 states within the same country.

Similarly, populations have fascinated me since I was a small child. Long before I could look such things up on the internet in five seconds, I had to wait to receive a yearly encyclopedia that included populations of important world metropolitan areas and see where my hometown (New York City) ranked. And I'm not the only person who cares about this sort of thing – upon visiting Mexico at age 10, my stepfather and a hotel employee had an odd moment where they compared city populations. We can talk more about Mexico in the Mexico chapter, but suffice it to say that one thing I noted was that, wherever it ranked, New York's metro area was always one of the world's most populous.

It's never been the biggest, though, at least since I started paying attention. Tokyo has always far outpaced NYC, with upwards of 40 million people in its metro area now, having had over 30 million since before I was born (World Population Review, 2025). I got curious years back to compare this to other locations I was familiar with, and, alongside California and Australia, both of which I'll get to in future chapters, one place I was interested in the relative population of was the country of Canada. I'll admit there was a petulance in my original interest; when teaching in South Korea, there was a strong contingent of Canadian teachers, and in fact I was told by a Korean colleague that the Canadian accent and 'look' – *which, yes, means 'white'* – was what they preferred to model for their students. This sort of annoyed me, because it's racist, but I didn't actually do anything about it besides trying to prove that not that many people live in Canada. And it's true.

Despite being the second-largest country on earth by land mass, Canada has approximately the same population as the Tokyo metropolitan area. Now, why am I telling this whole story here? Because perceptions of Canadian culture are driven by a relatively small number of people, most of whom live adjacent to the United States. In short, the way people see Canada – *and, for the purposes of this book, Canada's relationship to race and language* – is in direct contrast to the way we are viewed, and indeed, because they're considered 'nicer', they are presented as aspirational. I don't need to say much more to make the point that, though they're less aggressive than we are in their public personae, the idea that racism remains south of our border is nonsense, and it was important to me that I devote a chapter to what is clearly the largest geographical context I'll cover in this book – *I don't have a chapter on Russia* – to explore how our relationship shapes the way we minimize the raciolinguistic ideologies that continue to flourish in Canada.

And for the record, Canada is about 70% white (Statistics Canada, 2022), which is not *that* much more than the United States, but more importantly for my purposes, no other racial group comprises more than 7% of the population. Unlike the United States, English is only the first language of slightly more than half of the population, but (Canadian) French is second, which changes very little with regard to the dominance of colonial tongues.

Perception

People are 'nice' in Canada, and by comparison, people who are often – *but erroneously* – referred to as 'Americans' are rude and brash. Although there are regions within the United States that are considered relatively polite – *some of which we'll discuss on these pages* – compared to the way we present ourselves to the world through our media and – (*large sigh*) – our politicians. I'm somewhat referring to stereotypes, but in a way that's what this entire book is about, and as such, the question in this chapter is, essentially, are Canadians in fact nicer than the version of Americans propagated globally? Or, more specifically, is there less of an issue with harmful hierarchies being created and maintained through racism and language ideologies?

Above, I mentioned that I was told in South Korea that Canadian teachers were the 'ideal'. But let's unpack that – *I'm going to get tired of using that word eventually* – briefly before we dive into the interviews and other data. Canadians, despite their spelling, do not actually speak a British version of English, yet their languaging is still distinct from ours. Accents, sure, but also particular aspects of their vocabulary – *in the United States we'd say 'Ninth Grade' and they'd say 'Grade 9'* – are noticeable. It wouldn't be accurate to say it's a mix of the two in the sense of how and when their languaging developed, but as a member of the Commonwealth, which is therefore attached to the United Kingdom by history and other vestigial concepts, while also being literally attached to the United States by geography and treaty, Canada really does sit somewhat 'in between' the two nations, so to speak. With all that said, one of the primary differences between countries in Europe and those on what most refer to as the North American continent is who was there first. Namely, the fact that there were thriving cultures – *and languages* – present for centuries before the first Europeans arrived. Indeed, though there are other non-white races in Canada, even if not in exceptionally large numbers, what I want to focus on here is the country's treatment of its Indigenous population, as well as the populace's reaction to this history being quite literally uncovered.

Garcia (2021) explained as follows:

> The history of residential schools was cast into the spotlight with the discovery of the remains of 215 children in an unmarked gravesite near the Kamloops Residential School on Tk'emlúps te Secwépemc territories in British Columbia, Canada on May 27, 2021. The announcement of the findings triggered shock, trauma, and national mourning, drawing global attention to an ugly history from which many have shied away for decades. The news media uncovered layers of genocide by the perpetrators: governmental and religious institutions, along with their intentional dismantling of Indigenous identities to control retaliation of future generations. Residential schools are known as a dark history of Canada, but for many Indigenous Peoples, the repercussions continue into the present day. The uncovering of unmarked gravesites offers a mere glimpse of the impacts of genocide.

I am not a scholar who spends considerable time wallowing in discussions of genocide. I don't believe I should have to retraumatize my minoritized readers to convince white readers to care, which is also part of why I didn't spend all much time interviewing people of color about their painful experiences – ultimately, this book, and my scholarship writ large, is about whiteness. And you can Google my previous book for sad stories like those. Accordingly, I don't particularly plan to focus on the details of the mass graves, of which this was only one of many that continue to be uncovered. No, I want to zero in on one detail the author mentioned in the passage above; not the trauma or the mourning, but the 'shock'. To which I ask, *why?*

I contend that the stereotypes and perceptions I mentioned are a major contributing factor to a sense of shock, shock not just that these things occurred, but shock they occurred in *Canada*, the nicer Northern neighbor. As that same article explains, these graves were found on the site of a now-closed residential school, institutions that were created to 'separate Indigenous children from their families in order to weaken their cultural lineage and integrate them into a new colonial culture that formed Canadian society'. Linguistic destruction was a key feature of the practice, and the final school only closed in 1896, which is far too late. I'm sorry, I was wrong – it was 1996, when I was 10. Even the various reform schools to which many Black American children were sent were mostly shuttered long before that. If you were of Indigenous or First Nations heritage in Canada, this would have been extremely common knowledge. So again I ask, what is there to be shocked about if you were paying attention at all, or, is it only a certain segment of the country's population that was sequestered enough from said atrocities that their discovery could be considered shocking?

Additionally, for those outside of Canada, the perception that *this* country could have behaved just as brutally as the neighbor seen as the racist bully nation upends its constructed image. So in this chapter I want to try and unpack – *argh* – that image just a bit, as well as taking a moment to examine why it might be possible for Canadians of European descent, people who speak colonial languages and maintain their national dominance, to find what I must cynically call a mundane series of tragedies so shocking.

Reality

My friend Nella was someone I knew when I lived in South Korea. Unlike a lot of the non-Koreans I knew there, she has, like me, remained in education in various jobs over the last decade-plus, and occupies a unique racial position, wherein if you read her (real) name or she tells you about her background, you'd know she isn't exclusively white at all, but her partially Scottish heritage has made it such that she passes as white at first glance. This is a niche I've always found fascinating, people who are superficially racialized as white but know in their bones that they aren't – these people can access contexts that few can, where they can find themselves in what others believe are exclusively white spaces and hear an honest account of feelings, while having the perspective that comes from having a different background. How I wish I could disguise myself effectively to do research like this, but, well, that would probably involve garish makeup and no one would believe it. As she told me, 'most of my friends don't know exactly where I'm from', and, frankly, neither did I until she told me as part of this interview.

Regarding residential schools and the Canadian 'awakening' in education, she said the following:

> [After the final school closed in 1996], it took a decade for them to even apologize, and then another decade for anything to be actually concretely

done about it. So it's like we're still *in that*. And so now, it's actually being presented in schools in books to kids. Not in a way like it was to me. My generation, it was like, *'they were savages*. And these were the savages that lived here when the British came, or when the French came, and we had to civilize them. We have to teach them our ways.' That was what I grew up in. I wish I kept these books. So now they're being taught in a very different way, but this is only in the last few years that these books have changed, so people over a certain age are almost willingly trying to not read too much about it. Many teachers go out of their way to talk about it and share it with their students, but that's not the majority.

I suppose, based on that account, it's not a shock that there would be such shock around the country when these facts were revealed.

Now, in addition to shock, there's a right wing effort to debunk the discovery of said mass graves. Possibly because of the people who fund and control a lot of the internet these days, most of the results that appear when you try to do quick research about the 2021 discoveries are conservative publications – e.g. the New York Post, *which, I have no idea why they care about Canada* – trying to discredit the movement to support the communities involved. Yes, that's an American news outlet, but it's replicated in the country's own National Post, which has significant influence. I bring this up not to engage in or even entertain a debate about the veracity of the evidence, but to make two points.

First, regardless of what the subject is, if the harm visited upon a marginalized group isn't cataloged via traditional means – *say, academic or scientific journals* – the evidence is often discounted, despite the fact that these traditional means are controlled by the populations that created said harm. In other words, we believed what, say, slaveowning scholars said about slavery more than we believed the enslaved populations. I won't bother with this in every chapter but it's worth noting if you find yourself attempting to object to the evidence.

Second, Nella is not particularly old; when she's referring to her generation, it's the same as mine, and I'm 39 – *it's anonymized, Nella, you'll be okay*. The point being, teaching materials treating First Nations individuals as 'savages' is not a relic of history but in fact a recent phenomenon.

As she continued, giving advice to fellow educators:

You can introduce one story or like one play. Even on Truth and Reconciliation day, I made a PowerPoint for everyone to share with their students, just in case they're curious about it, send this to them. And teachers wrote to me complaining that they don't have time. They've already made their calendar, when are they supposed to teach this and I'm like, you don't even have to teach it. Just give it to them. And let them read it if they want to. I mean, you don't have to teach it, just present it if it's too much trouble and it was like, you know, I just stopped doing things. I mean, at a certain point, it's like they don't want to grow or learn or it makes them uncomfortable. And I think they'd rather just close their eyes to it, and the three or four who do, you know, do a lot and then go out of their way to try to increase awareness wherever however they can.

First, 'Truth and Reconciliation Day' is the holiday of mourning referred to in the earlier portion wear Canadians are meant to wear orange in recognition of the lives that were lost at residential schools, though if my own experience is any indication, telling a majority-white group that they can make a meaningful impact by wearing a certain color is unlikely to lead to more impactful behavior.

Additionally, those attitudes exhibited by Nella's colleagues, the reactions that stop short of actual vitriol but make it clear that change is not worth the effort, are not exactly, let's just call it, 'nice'. It brings to mind a constant debate in which I've engaged, whether the overt racism of racial slurs and the like is 'better' or 'worse' than behavior such as this, which contributes to ongoing oppression and hierarchies but does not evince actual hatred. I guess that's in the eye of the beholder, but I'd say that although the type of racism this book seeks to explore – *which is behavior like those of her colleagues* – may be less scary in the short-term because there's no bodily threat, but it's the refusal for majoritized individuals to experience discomfort that has been the biggest obstacle for me in my own career and life. Like I said, eye of the beholder, though.

As far as language is concerned, implied by the word 'savage' – *or any materials to that effect* – is a low level of intelligence and linguistic ability. Obviously to anyone reading this, Indigenous populations possess the ability to communicate via language, but it's not a *colonial* language, so to the invading populations it is invalid. Language, in a certain sense, is equated with civilization (Mills & Lefrancois, 2018), so there's no real distinction between assigning a group savage qualities and dismissing their linguistic value. This is particularly galling in a country such as Canada that is, far more so than the United States, respectful of a certain type of bilingualism, but of course it has to be the 'right' languages for this legitimacy to be conveyed and maintained.

To this point, Nella added the following:

There's this sort of impression I get, especially from a lot of Western European languages that aren't English, that racism is only within the English language. Right? Like you can only access racism if you are going to use English, and you're more susceptible to racist ideas and stuff like that. That's obviously not true. It's not like the policies that exclude areas, advocate groups, or whatever, or low numbers of people from different racial groups in positions of power is unique to the English speaking provinces. Right? So I find that that sort of it's just sort of a reluctance to take full stock of oneself as a group.

Oh, no, she found the not-so-secret thesis of my book, that the boogeyman of the American South – *or contemporary global right-wing politics* – and its mustache-twirling villainy is the source of all racism is a convenient scapegoat for quieter versions of race- and language-based bigotry. But shh.

I think what she said here is pretty interesting, and despite my own opinions, the elision of racism and English in this particular way is fascinating. It's not just a belief that racism is confined within imaginary national borders, but in fact the ideology that racism can *only be accessed via English*. Racism is not a secret chamber of the mind that is difficult to find, and it certainly didn't start within the English language. We can debate where our modern version of racism started, but many argue that both whiteness and racism, as we know them today, arose to help justify the Atlantic slave trade, and it sure wasn't anyone speaking English who originated that process (Painter, 2011).

Indeed, the more I hear from people in different contexts, the more I think that American boorishness and its downstream popular culture are doing an excellent job of taking the responsibility off of everyone else, and ensuring that, as Nella said, they never are forced to take full stock of themselves.

What Needs to Happen

I can go two directions with this, and maybe you can help me choose. The choice is really between pragmatism and justice. If we choose pragmatism, then the solution to Canada's racial and linguistic issues is simply honesty about their complicity. That's not necessarily a conclusion, but it's better than being shocked about what was fully supported and sponsored. On the other hand, the justice solution is to *stop* engaging in colonialist behavior, but perhaps that's fundamentally impossible in a member of the Commonwealth, if only by definition and status.

I don't believe that Canada should stop attempting to be seen as 'nice' – I am advocating for the country to, uh, *reconcile* with their behaviors and attempt to correct them beyond commemorating horror once a year. The outcomes for the Indigenous population of Canada are markedly inferior when compared to other residents (Durand-Moreau *et al.*, 2022), and I contend that the broader perception of the Canadian demeanor has a deleterious impact on their urgency to address their shortcomings. The cognitive dissonance of what ends up being viewed as a clash between niceness and cruelty can only cause immobility, so, whatever direction we choose, Canada needs to make actual movement towards being the place it would rather the rest of us believe it to be.

As Nella told me, 'It's very much people in power wanting to keep people in power in power and keep other people out of it and language is 100% the tool that's being used in this province right now.' As with many of the contexts I'll feature, Canada acts as though it celebrates languages and languaging that are outside of the mainstream, but simultaneously uses raciolinguistic ideologies to reify societal hierarchies. That previous sentence had a lot of academic vocabulary, but there's a reason for that – I'm trying to demonstrate that this harm is hidden behind intellectual superiority. In other words, it's harder to work against harm with it's linguistically obfuscated from the people receiving the harm.

Ultimately, Canada is a very large place that I haven't necessarily done comprehensive justice to, or treated fairly. But given the way it's behaved, despite its image, is it a place that requires any fairness? Or is it just a vestigial tail of colonialism? I think you know the answer.

Speaking of the Commonwealth, though, it's time we traveled to the very center thereof, the place that gives this language its name, and its infuriating inability to contend with the racial and linguistic harm it has wrought across the globe.

3 It's Time for the Sun to Set

The United Kingdom

Background

I'll start with the metrics this time: the UK is 84% white, with nothing else more than 7% of the population (Office of National Statistics, 2024). Now, I could make a joke here about the overcast weather making light-colored skin more common, but I won't, because I'm mature. No, I just want to point out that it's pretty hard to be measurably less diverse than Canada, but they have managed to do so. But maybe they should actually be proud of their current level of homogeneity, because it's an improvement over the 96% rate from 1981. Good for them.

Now, I perhaps should have saved this chapter for the end, really, because it's the beginning of all this English business, but it still fits here where it's been placed. The United Kingdom, in videogame parlance, is sort of the 'final boss' of the phenomenon I am trying to explore. Or, I should say, there are three intertwined phenomena, and the UK exemplifies one of them. The first is English-speaking parts of the United States and Canada that use the historical South and Jim Crow laws to flatter themselves while perpetuating the same structural racism in more subtle ways; the second is contexts in which the connection between language and racial hierarchies might appear not to be clear (e.g. upcoming chapters on East Asia and Algeria); and the third is contexts in which it's obvious, if you think about it for more than half a second, how complicit the people are in upholding said systems, but their physical location – *and psychological distance* – from where many of their misdeeds occurred makes it far easier for both everyday citizens and the individuals in the education/academia sphere to pretend these issues are either in the past or located elsewhere. And there is no place that exemplifies this third phenomenon as perfectly as the United Kingdom.

As of this writing, the actual landmass of what is considered the United Kingdom itself – *and not the other places it stole and retains* – is approximately 243,000 square kilometers (Office for National Statistics, 2024), a measure I'll use to fit the context I'm speaking about. By comparison, that size places it in between the US States of Michigan and Minnesota, which is not insubstantial, but given its global prominence, is still rather minuscule. If you're not from the United States and would prefer an international comparison, the UK sits snugly in between Guinea and Uganda on the global list, a fact I ironically learned from Encyclopedia Britannica (2024), which apparently still exists. That last comment there is a joke, but not really, in the sense that the UK is perhaps the most glaring example of a faded empire in actual landmass that retains (much of) its influence via soft power. The United States may yet lose its power if our politics continues to trend the way it has in recent years, but because the colonists – *oh hey, they were mostly from (what is now) the UK!* – managed to amass territories that were actually contiguous, no matter how much chaotic flailing we descend into, we are unlikely to actually physically shrink in a noticeable way, even if, say, Puerto Rico or the US Virgin Islands were to become independent nations. So, the UK is a series of relatively small islands that add up into a slightly above-median-size country, and here we are, writing and reading and publishing in *English* all the same.

I'm not going to spend this chapter providing too much of a history as to how English as a language gained its global stranglehold. You wouldn't be reading anything of mine if you were unaware. No, more than any other context on this list, the UK has an interesting position as the progenitor of the world's (still) dominant language, one that fits hand-in-glove with raciolinguistic ideologies and upholds rankings that are difficult to dislodge. At the same time, though, they are a country full of scholars and other thinkers challenging these issues, and I suspect that they will prove to have shown considerable effort towards unpacking their involvement in colonialism and linguistic imperialism. After all, if English is named after (a part of) their country, it ought to be them that helps dismantle the structures it has built. Right?

...Right?

Perception

I sort of gave away the game up above, but at the core of this book's analysis is that the American South feels like the most 'real' racism to many, for reasons I've repeated and will repeat again. One of said reasons, of course, is the undeniable fact that the American South is a – *though not the only* – primary site of chattel slavery's results. There is still denialism of the brutality of the enterprise, but it's very hard to argue against the reality that that plantation is right over there, and that it was only a few generations ago for many Black Americans – *myself included* – that their ancestors were enslaved in these environs. The American Civil War was fought over the preservation of the institution; despite some, who shall not be cited, who would argue it was for 'states' rights', it was the states' rights to continue to perpetuate slavery that was the primary issue of contention.

Now, the fact that there were no longer slaves in (most of) the other existing states is often transmogrified into believing that there were never slaves in New York or Massachusetts, and that's just not true (see Painter, 2011 for more on all this). But, growing up in New York, even as a descendant of enslaved people, it was natural to create a mental distance from what the South represented, and that was on the same land mass. So, to bring us to the subject of this chapter, then, imagine having an entire ocean between yourself and the harm your nation has wrought. Even if your heart is in the right place, so to speak, through no fault of your own, and through the concerted efforts of those who would rather this be the case, you can truly believe your country lacks complicity in the overall enterprise in question, which in this case is the discomfiting reality that having centuries of 'successful' settler colonialism on stolen land required the imported labor represented by stolen humans.

If there's a common perception of the UK with respect to this sort of harm, it is probably that 'they're better than they used to be'. Consider how many territories have gained their (nominal) independence since the 18th century – the UK holds the Guinness world record for 'most countries to have gained independence from a single country' (Guiness, 2024), which I'm not sure is something to be proud of exactly, but I suppose it's better than continuing to own them. There are, as of this writing, 65 countries on that A(fghanistan) to Z(imbabwe) list, and considering there are around 200 independent nations currently, that's a third of the planet! So, in other words, *at least they're not how they used to be*, one might believe.

Regarding the Atlantic slave trade, there is also the fact that the UK chose to end its participation before the United States did, and while that *is* true, the date on which slavery was abolished depends on how charitable you'd like to be toward the Empire. They outlawed the trading of slaves in 1807 – good! But all the extant slaves on their many, many colonies were still in bondage. Not good. In 1833, they finally decreed these individuals would be free – good! But only technically as of the following summer … and also slave owners – *including members of parliament, of course* – would be heavily compensated … and also it excluded the East India Company territories. That is a few too many caveats for my taste.

And then finally, there is the simple problem of, to use their terminology, maths. More specifically, even if we give them credit for 1807 – *and we shouldn't, but let's just say we did* – they started in 1562. Now, the United States wasn't a country until 1776, when they gained independence from … someone, but, to be the most *un*charitable to the timeline on this side of the Atlantic, you can count from 1619 to 1865.

1807–1562 = 245
1865–1619 = 246

One year less, with the most charitable possible interpretation. What an incredible moral victory!

I hope you can see what I'm getting at, and I by no means am letting the United States off the hook for the way they've used prisoners as a proxy for slave labor in the century-plus since 1865, but that's not unique to us. Suffice it to say, even bending over backward to give the UK credit, they're not actually all that much 'better' than their boorish little brother, and that's without considering that they didn't exactly happily walk away from all 65 of those countries, on top of the destruction wrought by their, and other colonial nations', haphazard partitioning of said territories in the first place.

And we didn't even talk about the linguistic arm of their imperialist behavior yet. But we'll get there.

Reality

'There is that narrative that what's gone is gone', Dr. Peter Malcolm, who researches language and race in the UK, told me when I interviewed him. 'You know, what is the colonial past is the past and like, we recognize that some bad things happened, but, you know, we've moved on from there.

'I mean, you look at the way that schools for example ignore and downplay the role of British colonialism and the transatlantic slave trade. And this slight increasing pushback ... to have those discussions about colonialism and colonialism and slavery within the curriculum in education. And like this kind of fear, that bringing up and digging up the past is going to be somehow damaging to children's own perceptions of our brain and the way that kids from a super young age in this country get socialized into these nationalistic ideologies, about which language plays a central part.'

Dr. Malcolm and I once competed for an award, and he was named the victor, but if anyone was going to beat me, I was glad it was him, because he's one of the few scholars in the UK that I've found with the honesty to contend with how English upholds this denial we're discussing here.

Another friend and intellectual colleague of mine is Dexter Herz, who has been teaching in the field for about a decade.

'I think when I started working in [English for Academic Purposes]', he explained, 'I think you really come across a lot of deficit narrative about students, thinking that they're not capable of doing things. Like a common example is if they're Chinese and they "can't do" critical thinking. And even just very subtle things, like calling the students "chickens." It's supposed to be in a nice way ... I think, that whole deficit mindset is connected to, to racism and you know, kind of like having a colonial idea about students as well. And it's really, really complex. And so I just started to try and explore it a bit more.'

Dr. Malcolm actually challenged one of my own perceptions from the section above – *and I know some of you were already sending me an angry email about it; that's why it's called 'perceptions'* – in telling me, to my own surprise, 'We like to think of this thing that, of course, we were *involved in* but, British people like to think of it as being spatially distant and geographically distant and therefore ideologically distant, but there were slaves right here in Britain, and that history of slavery is so ignored in the British consciousness, and the education system and there is that narrative that what's gone is gone.' To pat myself on the back, though, if it's ignored in *British* education, then imagine how little of that information has made it across to our own shoddy history books. We barely acknowledge the sundown towns in our backyard.

He continued, drawing a direct connection from the history and proliferation of English to the colonialism the country would prefer not to discuss.

> What was unique about Britain is that language discrimination and language hierarchy, or stratification or whatever you want to call it, was a design feature of British colonialism. Right? The punishment of Indigenous languages, of Black African languages, of non European languages. The eradication of non European languages and entire lifeworlds was a means to how the British justified their colonial project. So, when we talk about the co-construction of race and class and language, that co-construction was so normalized within the British colonial project. And that co-construction then gave rise to genocide, the stealing of land, cultural eradication, enslavement, et cetera. And perceptions about language was so, so central to those activities. So if you look at early kind of forms of British 'travel writing', when you had British colonizers documenting what they were seeing and what they were perceiving and what they were encountering, within these, like, exotic worlds that they were, you know, arriving uninvited to, what you see is that perceptions of language plays such a central part in the way that those populations were dehumanized. And this was going on from the late 1400s onwards, through to the mid-1800s. And those processes of dehumanization were integral to that colonial project.

Let's add some gristle to this for the readers who would dispute his statements.

First, yes there were slaves in Britain (Olosuga, 2015). And second, 'travel writing' was indeed a political effort of imperialism, especially seeing as how most of the public could not read or afford to take a holiday, and as such the accounts were mostly being shared among the wealthy, from their superior vantage point (Hulme & Youngs, 2002). What you may best know as the realm of a *Lonely Planet* series is just the diluted version of this practice, thankfully now somewhat more democratized and not solely controlled by those seeking to invade a new space – *though it's not as different as it should be if you've read those Lonely Planet books.*

Dr. Malcolm had a lot to share about the subject, understandably:

> I've lost count of the number of times where I've done talks or papers reviewed in the peer review system or wherever. And the response so many times has been, 'Why are you talking so much about race and colonialism? Where's this come from? Why is this relevant? You're talking about things that have happened in the past! You're talking about things that are centuries ago.' As if coloniality and colonial logics that were so central to British colonialism have now somehow dissipated and somehow disappeared. And that those colonial ideologies about language that were so central, that were that design feature of British colonialism are somehow now not relevant to language and education and the disciplines of applied and sociolinguistics. So that it's always been really troubling to me as somebody that lives and works within, arguably the world's most powerful language empire, like the seeds of where that empire in that global linguistic project came from, especially as a white person researching these things. Because it was white people that produced those ideologies. It was white people that co-constructed those taxonomies and those hierarchies. So, that concern and that worry is something that I tried to send so much in my work both as a reaction to what I saw not happening from my other colleagues, but also as just a refusal to separate out those things like the historical facts about language and colonialism within Britain and the way in which they absolutely shape society, and especially schools today.

I can't directly cite his work here without giving away his identity, but suffice it to say he's one of the most prominent younger scholars in the top in the UK, and the country would be better off heeding his warnings. My confidence that they will do so is not particularly high.

Dexter's particular experience has helped him understand the contrasting perspectives of the United States and the UK with regard to racism and language, and he compared them accordingly:

> You do see extreme examples of racism in the US but I also think when you look at the scholarly work, and just the general population, I think, are much better at talking about race and racism than we are in the UK. Yeah, we haven't had to deal with it as much, I think in the last few years in Black Lives Matter and, George Floyd all of those conversations have been happening more. But at the same, the idea that it's not relevant in the UK is kind of ridiculous. There's loads and loads of stuff written about it in the UK as well and there's loads of films about it. And in the 1970s, and 80s and Windrush and and Grenfell, there's so

much going on in the UK, so it's the idea that this is an American thing is just ridiculous.

'Windrush' (Rawlinson, 2018) and 'Grenfell' (Block, 2019) are both scandals that exemplify the sort of racism that circulates the globe under the radar. Very few racial slurs are uttered, no white hoods are donned, but if (in the former case), a few people die after being wrongly deported and they happen to be people of color, so be it. If (in the latter) a large number of people die because of lax maintenance and other negligence, and they happen to predominantly have immigrated from impoverished – *and non-white* – countries, so be it. It's a lot easier for racist *impact* to occur when you cannot admit to an institutional racist intent.

He mentioned how he'd tried to use one of my recorded talks in his class and found strong objections to it. At first, it was complaints about my casual nature and my approach, which, whatever – I want to get to what he thinks was truly leading to the animosity.

'One of the things', he explained, 'was they didn't like this kind of critical race theory, racial discourse coming into that precessional because that resistance was beyond where they can see the students like chickens. The other thing was, well, I think they had a problem with your identity as a Black American. Basically. That's what I think it was about.'

Don't anyone reading this worry about British people I've never met being somewhat exclusionary toward me. The point is that the racism in the UK is couched inside of language, as well as a refusal to grapple with a provable reality, and many people in the country suffer accordingly.

What Needs to Happen

How do you solve a problem like ~~Maria~~ the namesake of the English language, the former owner of much of the world, and the country that is trying to hold onto its faded power by any means necessary? I'm not sure you can.

Even if the UK's official landmass continues to shrink and makes its name more and more amusing – *there's not a lot of stuff that remains 'united' after all* – so long as there is a London, and so long as there is an English, they cannot be dismissed or ignored. The general suggestions made by Dr. Malcolm are the ideal, that the schools change paths and actually teach real history about what crimes the country has committed, but those suggestions are true in almost every context I'm covering here and are not at all unique to the UK.

There's a popular meme that flies around social media on occasion, which is sourced from a British sketch comedy show called *That Mitchell and Webb Look*. I confess a general ignorance of the preponderance of British sketch comedy shows, as, given their shorter tenure compared to

American series, there seem to be just so many that I can't keep up. But I know this meme.

Accordingly, the scholarly journal – *I joke, but more people have read it than will ever read this, or attend any conference at which one of us speak* – Know Your Meme describes the scene as follows:

> [The meme] is from a sketch by the British comedy show *That Mitchell and Webb Look* in which two men play Nazis who realize they're the 'bad guys' of World War II. The line has been used as a reaction image to situations where a person who identifies with a cause or group realizes their aims may not be good. (Know Your Meme, 2024)

I am sure some of you know the meme I am referring to by now. It's meant to be humorous in the sketch, and of course I can't paint the UK as equivalent to Nazis, but I think it's a legitimate avenue of resolution for what the country can do, nay must do, if they ever want to counteract what has occurred over the past several centuries. There's no true way to accurately repair colonialism – giving up various nations is nice, I suppose, but it doesn't undo what was done to them before that date. No, the shift that is necessary is purely ideological. As Dr. Malcolm says, schoolchildren are 'socialized into these nationalistic ideologies', and I am putting forth that a shift in this mindset is the only way to untangle the knot that the UK has wrought. In short, as the meme puts forth, the UK, from its institutions to its people, needs to ask itself, 'Are we the baddies?' And then, whatever answer it reaches, it needs to honestly explore what led them to the present day.

Oh? What's that? The UK commissioned a government report on racism in recent years? That's a great first step. Let's see what they said:

> This report speaks to a new period, which we have described as the era of 'participation'. We can only speak of 'participation' if we acknowledge that the UK has fundamentally shifted since those periods in the past and has become a more open society. We have spoken in this report about how the UK is open to all its communities. But we are acutely aware that the door may be only half open to some, including the White working class. In this regard we have pointed out how in education, employment, health and crime and policing the UK can be a more inclusive and fairer landscape.
>
> Participation, however, is not just about fully opening the doors, we also speak to the need for communities to run through them and grasp those opportunities. We have found that some ethnic minorities have been able to 'participate' better than others. We were impressed by the 'immigrant optimism' of some of the new African communities. They are among the new high achievers in our education system. As their

Caribbean peers sit in the same classrooms, it is difficult to blame racism in education for the latter's underachievement. (UK Government, 2021)

Hmm. Let's review.

'The UK has fundamentally shifted since those periods in the past and has become a more open society.'

'We also speak to the need for communities to run through them and grasp those opportunities.'

'As their Caribbean peers sit in the same classrooms, it is difficult to blame racism in education for the latter's underachievement.'

Look, you can find the rest of the report online, as it's publicly available, but if you've read this far into my book, I'm not sure I need to explain to you what the issues are with what's being asserted. Suffice it to say that the UK government itself doesn't seem to have entertained the idea that they could, in fact, be the baddies, and they're never going to be the country they believe themselves to be until they do so.

4 Jim Croc

Australia

Background

Look, I assure you we will escape from the Commonwealth soon enough, but we're not done just quite yet.

Australia is an interesting case. I feel like, depending on your age and location, its stereotypes vary from sundry outback tropes to those that reflect the more urban areas that dot the coasts. When it comes to what we're discussing here, though, I'm not sure I would have been able to tell you about its racial and linguistic diversity before looking it up. Australia – *well, Oceania* – is the only (populated) continent I've never visited in any capacity, though I got very close in Indonesia once, which I realize, as I edit this, that I already said, but, oh well. Not that I am claiming to be an expert on any of the places covered in this book aside from the final chapter on New York, but I truthfully cannot make any claims on having personally experienced racism in Australia whereas I can absolutely do so in the Pacific Northwest, or Western Europe, or East Asia.

Linguistically, Australia is more diverse than its progenitors in the United Kingdom, with around three-quarters of the country asserting that they speak only English. It's interesting to see how that very source – *the World Atlas (2024)* – describes how this came to be though. As they wrote, 'Early European settlement in Australia almost eradicated the indigenous languages, and few of these aboriginal languages have survived today.' Interesting juxtaposition of diction there, I would say. To be clear, I am not necessarily buying the claim that aboriginal languages have vanished, and this will be touched upon in the interview text later, but even if that were true, they accurately describe this violent process as 'eradication' while softening it with 'European settlement'. This is just some generic, albeit well-sourced, statistics website, not a leading publication or an academic journal, but these words matter and their uneasy coexistence in the same sentence feels pointed to someone who pays far too much to such things like me (and probably you).

Switching over to race, which is certainly understood *differently* there – *although we'll discuss the persistence of white supremacy all the same* – Australia is significantly less homogenous than the other Commonwealth nations we've visited thus far. Obviously all of these numbers are estimates, but only about 68% of Australians are of European (or Australian) descent (Migration Policy Institute, 2024). Adding in a handful of others from the Americas and the like, you still have a country that is significantly more diverse, in every meaningful sense, than Canada and the UK, and while those aren't exactly the highest bars to clear, it's not nothing.

So essentially, we have a country that is almost exactly the same size as the contiguous United States – *Alaska is doing a lot of work for our overall girth over here* – but that is, by both definition and bodies of water, discrete from much of the rest of the world. Obviously, with the internet, the world is much 'smaller' but raciolinguistic ideologies are far older than social media, so this is an exercise in briefly investigating how our hierarchies have and haven't traveled to the other side of the planet.

Perception

I admit I really had no idea how Australia dealt with race, aside from being fairly certain that their settler colonialism was sadly standard. Most of the Australians I've met, between my time in South Korea, the few who've made it all the way to New York and others I encountered when I was a 20-something who thought hostels were 'cool', didn't stray too far from the stereotypes I already mentioned. Not so much the outback per se, but there was a persistent – *and insistent* – relaxed nature and demeanor. Indeed, though I wasn't yet the academic bore I've aged into, I still occasionally brought up at least superficial politics if they felt relevant, and there was no group of people less interested in such discussions, particularly if various minoritized identities were involved. They were very friendly to me otherwise, but it did feel as though there was a limit to the space I was allowed to occupy. Is that racism? Not necessarily; I don't doubt they would have rolled their eyes at a white American talking about 'issues'. The point I am making is that the vibe I felt – *and it was definitely a vibe more than anything else* – was that they just wanted to be able to, as the kids used to say, chill out, and anything too serious would, as the kids have definitely stopped saying by now, yuck their yum, or ruin the fun they were intent on having.

But they're not here right now so let's ruin their fun.

The only thing I knew about Australia and race before this work was their almost predictable treatment of their Indigenous population. I didn't know the details, but I knew they'd done what other settler colonialists had done in turning what was decidedly not a white space into one that looked very different. I did wonder if the particulars had been different given the relatively harsh terrain of the country's interior, but then I remembered that Canada doesn't exactly have the most favorable conditions once you leave the border with the United States and they still managed to steal all that land all the same.

Now, most people know that what we know of as Australia 'started' – *though again there were whole societies already in place* – as an outpost for criminals sent away from the United Kingdom (and Ireland), over 160,000 thereof between the late 18th century and throughout the 19th century (National Library of Australia, 2024). Australia, even to this day, still has a relatively small population for its size – *it's not quite as sparsely populated as Canada, but it's close* – so, when so many of the 'settlers' were actually descended from populations considered 'undesirable', it paints a particular picture of the people in the place. Of course, eventually a so-called modern and advanced society was constructed, so this helps create an image of a group of people who emerged from chaos into something more similar to what we'd 'expect' out of a Western Europe or United States. The association with criminality is a badge of pride, the same way the United States lionizes 'wild west' outlaws and 'explorers', none of whom participated in harmful colonist behavior, none at all. The past criminality of the (white) Australian population is therefore part of this country's, as mentioned before, master narrative, and the more recent stereotypes of Steve Irwin–types living among dangerous wildlife is merely a diluted version of these same cultural myths and tropes, though by all accounts Irwin was a very nice man, so no offense meant to him and his memory. Anyway, to an outsider like me, the entirety of Australia is erroneously portrayed as a currently extant version of the Wild West, and if there's one thing our own stories about the Wild West ignored, it was our treatment of the people who were already there.

But we're not really focused on the past here insomuch as how it influences current perceptions, so let's talk about the way majoritized Australians portray Aboriginal people. From Creative Spirits (2024), which documents current Aboriginal issues in the country, we have the following excerpt about the tourism industry, which further excerpts text published by the official Australian tourism entity:

'The tourism industry has perfected the art of creating the good stereotype in the minds of readers of their promotional material without saying anything that's untrue. Read the following extract of a text by Tourism Australia which appeared in a German newsletter about Australia:

> *The Aborigines of Australia are the keepers of one of the oldest existing cultures. They are proud of their culture and traditions. They love to share their traditional music, ritual dances and knowledge about their land. Tourists who let themselves into meeting Aborigines during a tour into the outback can visit unique places, sense the spirituality of ancient customs, experience the spectacular nature or get close to how these people live during a stay in an Aboriginal community.*

> *You meet Aboriginal art and culture everywhere in Australia. If along the coast, in the heart of Australia or even at Circular Quay in Sydney or the Botanic Gardens of Melbourne – Aboriginal art and culture is present in the entire country. Tourists have many options to experience it. In urban regions, for example, galleries and exhibitions offer views into contemporary Aboriginal Australia.*

'Analyzing the text we find words and attributes such as 'keepers', 'oldest', 'traditions', 'ritual' and 'ancient'. The text serves the stereotype of Aboriginal people 'living a traditional tribal/ancient lifestyle' mentioned earlier. It's all in the words. 'Contemporary' is only mentioned in conjunction with galleries and exhibitions. 95% of Australian tourists want to experience Aboriginal culture during their trip and that's why Tourism Australia has chosen to feature the image of an Aboriginal tour guide prominently on their website. But I have to disappoint you. Many Aboriginal people struggle to get jobs, even in the tourism industry. Some Aboriginal people might not even know about their own culture, have lost their family ties or don't practise any traditional customs at all.'

'Funny' is the wrong word for what I'm about to say, but it sure is interesting, at least, that Australia can be as physically distant as possible from most of the countries on this planet that are predominantly white, but that they have engaged in not just the same behaviors in the past, but also the exact same racist stereotyping that you see in any location hoping to attract wealthy – *and usually white* – Westerners for a visit. But this doesn't really tell us anything novel about the country's policies and practices – indeed it just makes Australia seem quite the same as the rest of the Commonwealth, which might be surprising to some, but isn't a 'revelation' worthy of this chapter. I'll need more than that to be taken aback.

Reality

'Are you familiar with the White Australia policy?'
I was not!
This question was asked to me while I interviewed Ronnie Carraway, an Australian educator. They shed light on something that I would assume most Australians are well aware of and yet, unlike the pop culture and master narratives of the American South that inspired this book, 'white Australia' sure hasn't made it too far beyond their shores.
As Ronnie explained:

Australia has a significant denial thing going on. And it is worth noting, very few Australians would deny perhaps that Trump and Boris Johnson represented some very significantly racialized policies. But both Donald Trump and Boris Johnson have name-checked Australia as inspirations for some of their policies, in particular things involving locking immigrants overseas to prevent them from being able to claim refugee status. And a lot of this is often tied up with linguistic questions as well. It's never gone away ... again, it's never framed as we're being racist. It is 'we're protecting our culture. We're protecting our language'.

Regarding the 'White Australia' policy, the National Museum of Australia describes it accordingly:

When Australia federated in 1901, parliamentarians felt it necessary to create a national law for immigration. The Immigration Restriction Bill was one of the first Bills introduced to the new parliament and proposed a twofold approach to restricting non-white population growth. The Act came into law on 23 December 1901. The Act gave immigration officers the power to make any non-European migrant sit a 50-word dictation test. This was initially given in any European language, and after 1905 in any prescribed language. As the language chosen for the dictation test was at the discretion of the immigration officer, it was easy to ensure failure for migrants deemed undesirable, either because of their country of origin, possible criminal record, medical history, or if considered morally unfit. Extremely small numbers of non-white migrants were ever allowed to pass. The test was administered 1,359 times prior to 1909, with only 52 people granted entry to Australia. After 1909 not a single migrant made to sit the test passed. Small numbers of migrants were granted certificates of exemption from the test but often exempted people became separated from their friends and family members who did not pass and were deported. The introduction of two accompanying acts (the *Pacific Island Labourers Act 1901* and the *Post and Telegraph Act 1901*) further limited access to Australia for non-white migrants by outlawing the use of imported labour and making it mandatory to hire white workers on any vessels transporting Australian mail. (National Museum of Australia, 2024)

Before I analyze the details above, I wanted to note that, although it has surpassed the UK in diversity, these policies had an immediate and lasting impact on the country's demographics, lowering the percentage of non-UK/Irish descent Australians to only 2.7% by 1947. These laws were eventually repealed in the late 20th century, but by then the damage was done. However, that's not really what I want to focus on.

In the middle of that passage, there's a key detail that crystalizes my overall thesis. To repeat briefly, 'The Act gave immigration officers the power to make any non-European migrant sit a 50-word dictation test. This was initially given in any European language, and after 1905 in any prescribed language. As the language chosen for the dictation test was at the discretion of the immigration officer, it was easy to ensure failure for migrants deemed undesirable, either because of their country of origin, possible criminal record, medical history, or if considered morally unfit.' Now, my argument is that the narrative of the American South exemplifying racism and thereby rendering others less severe despite their upholding the same hierarchical structures is hereby bolstered by the similarities between this policy and the processes that prevented Black Americans from voting in that same American South. For the unfamiliar, in states such as Mississippi and Alabama, a vital tool in diminishing the political power of Black residents was the creation of 'literacy tests'. Most of the questions were civics-related, the type you might find on a high school history exam – e.g. '*Name two of the purposes of the U.S. Constitution*' – but for a group that was not allowed to actually attend general public schools, the powers that be were well aware that they would struggle to pass, and struggle to pass they did. Tell me if the following numbers sound similar to the demographic impacts caused by the white Australia policy:

> In 1900, 100,000 African Americans were enrolled as voters in Alabama, but by 1908, only 3,742 were registered to vote. The Alabama Supreme Court adjusted the administration of the literacy test by introducing multiple versions with the intention of rendering it more challenging for African American voters to prepare adequately. From 1964 onwards, there were a total of 100 different versions of the test. (Ferris State University, 2023)

So, in precisely the same time period that the actual Jim Crow South was hard at work enforcing its racist structures, Australia wasn't behaving any better, and was receiving the same results. Interesting. We can call it *Jim Croc*.

Before you point out, as people tend to, that these sorts of things are in the past, Ronnie made clear the ongoing impact of these ideologies. As they told me,

> So we've continued something like [white Australia]. To get certain visas in Australia, you need to engage in English language tests through the English language industry. So you know, IELTS, though I will say I have previously worked for one of those companies, and that is something that I am honestly ashamed of now. Because once you see what is actually going on, it's pretty unpleasant. Again, this is always framed as, 'we are just protecting the rights of these immigrants to make sure that they are able to communicate appropriately in our society,' but it is actually very much a way of putting brakes on people seeking their visa rights. And it has been framed this way multiple times in the discourse by certain politicians, particularly conservative politicians, but it is worth noting, a lot of these processes were put in by our progressive governments as well, who have been quite full on pursuing these policies.

Their point about progressive politicians behaving similarly to conservative ones rings quite true from a US perspective. Setting aside our most odious figureheads, it is, somehow, American gospel that we need to 'limit' immigration and patrol the borders, but once you agree with this basic premise and cede this ideological territory, it's pretty hard to argue against the harsh tactics used to accomplish these goals. And to think I wrote that paragraph before the events of 2025, but anyway.

Ronnie tied the whole thing into a neat, ugly bow by making clear how race and language cannot be pulled apart from one another in Australia when it comes to their hierarchical structures.

> In Australia, it is still very, very acceptable to discriminate against people on the basis of their language or dialect. It is not considered the same as being racist. And I mean socially acceptable. Usually people do it explicitly and publicly, and the same people who would be absolutely horrified if somebody said something that they would consider racist, will nonetheless say, 'why don't they learn to speak English properly,' or, and I've heard teachers say this, as well in the staff room. And this carries us off to how indigenous languages are treated as well. In particular, we have a variety of English called Aboriginal English, which is considered a series of dialects and they are in many ways, very distinct from standard mainstream Australian English.... So as soon as I saw this [at the time recent] press conference with a translator speaking Aboriginal English, this was something I actually saw on Twitter. 'Why don't they speak the proper Australian language of English?' And, you know, there were the more benign comments, but it did get a lot nastier than that. And I heard this, even from other language teachers, they were often not aware that Aboriginal English is really quite a distinct series of dialects. And that itself varies from state to state, Western Australia and Northern Territory have much stronger representation of both their indigenous languages than other states like Victoria and New South Wales. Those languages really did suffer far more significantly from colonization to the extent that most of them have vanished. There are some rehabilitation efforts or revitalization efforts for a lot of them. But quite a lot of those languages' cultural knowledge, everything has vanished and that was often part of the official policy, removing languages were an official policy.... You see the same stories pop up over and over and over again. And often quite violent, quite horrific. Very similar tactics. Lots of separating children from their families. So yeah, Australia did that with quite a lot of gusto. And there is a huge denial about it in society, a lot of people refuse to believe that it's true. We've had academics who have published books claiming this is a myth. The usual, which again, from what I see in the discourse is very similar to what we often see in US discourse or UK discourse, which is, 'Hey, yeah, we may have got rid of the language but think of how much they gained! Their colonization has been a net gain for them.'

Sounds quite ... American if you ask me.

What Needs to Happen

In addition to curtailing their harmful practices, which I could say about any of these places, Australia needs to stop coasting on their carefree global reputation. Americans are seen as violent brutes, and that's not exactly untrue, but by comparison, the way many of the Commonwealth nations portray themselves belies their complicity in both settler colonialism and the upholding of white supremacy via linguistic ideologies and imperialism. In a way, it seems like the United States are their convenient scapegoat for the perpetuation of racism. And don't take it from me, take it from Ronnie:

> We have a whole big element of civil rights, which almost always focuses on US Civil Rights, very rarely on the situation in Australia. We talk about suffrage in Australia, the right to vote for women, we very rarely talk about indigenous rights. We learned about the Scottsboro boys. And again, that was something I've seen people from the USA, that they never heard mentioned or never learned about, and this surprises me. So as an Australian, it's really easy to think, 'I get it. Look, we even know better about the US history than the people from the US therefore we must be progressive.' But that is a way of framing us as being, I think, more progressive than the US while ignoring our own situation. And I can't help but feel it's deliberate.

It certainly seems that way. The question I have is, if the United States were to stop dominating global news and popular culture, what would Australia be left with in considering the persistence of racism? It's a thought experiment that's impossible to prove or disprove, but I can't help but wonder if they'd be forced to examine their own practices without a convenient, and incorrect, excuse that they're not as bad as we are.

5 The Purveyors of Public Pedagogy

California

Background

I told you we'd be leaving the Commonwealth eventually. Anyway, the challenge with this chapter is how to situate California alongside the Pacific Northwest – *which borders it to the north* – and a later chapter on Mexico. At the same time, one of the background themes of this book is the way popular culture shapes our views of what 'racism' is, and if there's a place from which much of said popular culture originates, it's certainly the state that contains Hollywood (and also Silicon Valley). Chances are, especially if you're not from the United States, your view of American racism has been shaped by people living and working in California; if the United State's faltering empire is centered in Washington, D.C., our soft power persists from the West Coast. We shape global perceptions of many topics through the media we generate, and that absolutely includes What Racism Is.

We've spent a few chapters in places that have fewer people than you might have assumed (e.g. Canada, Australia, maybe even the Pacific Northwest), and while there are sparsely populated regions of California for certain, there are more residents than you could have assumed. Were it its own country – *and ignoring that the population of the United States would be lower and screw up the rankings, but bear with me* – California would rank only slightly lower than Canada, and far ahead of Australia, despite being much smaller than either massive country. It is also our first example of what is awkwardly referred to as a 'majority-minority' state (US Census, 2023), which, for the purposes of the United States, means that white residents are less than half of the populace. Of course, people of European descent are not the native residents of any part of the United States, so a place like California underlines what I was referring to way back in the introduction with the word *minoritized*. You could say, in a very superficial manner, that people of Hispanic descent are not 'minorities' in California, but that hardly means they possess all of the societal power their presence might imply. Accordingly, I find this state, well known for progressive ideals and left-leaning films in recent decades, to be a useful exemplar of why just having more non-white residents doesn't inherently preclude racism and harmful linguistic ideologies.

At the same time, as I mentioned, California is also home to Silicon Valley and the cartoonish wealth disparity visible throughout the San Francisco Bay Area. On the one hand, there are many languages, races and cultures living near one another through the state, but in other ways, it might be one of the most unequal parts of the country, depending on how you define the term. If you don't look particularly closely, California can be seen as a pluralistic success story in contrast to the racism that many of us are most familiar with. But, well, you've read enough by now to know that that surely isn't true, so let's look and see what's actually going on in the Golden State.

Perception

I realized as I was about to put pen to paper – *well, fingers to keyboard* – that I'd already spent some time interviewing people about race and California when I was working on my dissertation. Consequently, any 'perception' I had before starting this book was assuredly influenced by those stories, so it would be silly for me not to share what I'd already learned. The following, then, is some excerpts from that work, followed by an analysis of how that does or doesn't reflect the perceptions of the Californian context.

> Many of the [dissertation] participants mentioned learning vaguely about race and racism but without hearing much of anything specific about the concepts. They recalled learning about the value of a nebulous version of equality but were never taught much beyond warm, superficial platitudes ... Kim is an interesting case because, while I knew her long before I taught the course, I actually knew nothing about her at all. We went to college together, but for whatever reason, we were not close, and I did not even know where she was from. Speaking of her background, then, she was born and raised in California, in an area she described as follows: 'Very deeply blue, very Democratic, very progressive, and yet also very wealthy. And so I grew up in an environment where the rhetoric was all about equality, and inclusivity, and trying to create opportunities for all sorts of people, but you would look around and not see all those sorts of people represented.' Her well-funded public high school had a handful of 'popular' students of color, but ... these classmates came from particular class backgrounds, and this allowed her peers to mostly convince themselves that they were already on the right path in that common, color-evasive way. (Gerald, 2022b)

Let's speak more directly about 'color-evasiveness' then. Until somewhat recently, it was more common to refer to this phenomenon as 'colorblindness', as implied the refrain, 'I don't see color.' Calling it 'colorblindness', though, has two issues. First, it's ableist, as it equates their behavior with a condition that is absolutely not a choice whatsoever; and second, as I just referenced, what people are doing with regard to race and racism is not being *unable* to see said differences but actively choosing to look away from them (see, among others, Zamudio & Rios, 2006, for more). To be clear, color-evasive racism is still racism, even if it doesn't contain any slurs, you could say that this entire book is about color-evasiveness in some fashion, though the particular case of California is an example of a context in which they proudly proclaim their progressiveness, similar to the Pacific Northwest but with a much more diverse population.

Returning to the prior research conducted:

> These participants all learned, I would argue, about what Bonilla-Silva (2017) would call *racism without racists*, or, alternatively, understanding that racism exists but is distant from one's life and context, located in a different era or location, which also allows for the othering discourse in evidence above to be seen as divorced from the system of racism. I would also put myself in this category, based on what I was taught in school, since, although my parents were very clear about our own identity, it was my institutions that I unfortunately listened to on the subject. I should add, however, that ... even if they had been taught more explicitly about racism, it might have remained divorced from the institutional forces that uphold it – they were taught that racism was based in interpersonal interactions in other locations, and instead of learning that racism was present in their own lives from particular bad actors, what they ought to have learned was the more subtle ways that the system is upheld.

This final series of points here is fairly complex, so I want to pause and – *eyeroll at self* – unpack it. For someone in California, inside of the American context but separated from experiencing racism directly, either because of racial or class privilege, or both, it probably wouldn't be enough merely to be taught that racism is present in their location rather than just in, say, the American South. They also needed to be taught that racism in their location was structural rather than contained within 'bad actors' they live alongside. Think about what we've discussed thus far – racism in Australia is the 'white Australia' policy as much as or moreso than yelling at someone of a different color. But if Kim, an academic who is probably even more educated than I am, was two levels of awareness away from a clear-eyed understanding of Californian racism, then what hope does someone have in other locations much farther removed?

A final excerpt worth discussing:

Here one can see the distance between talk and action, the 'rhetoric' Kim referred to leading to no substantive changes. This amorphous understanding of racism as a bad-but-distant thing helped generate white savior mindsets in several of the participants, and in fact this mindset was partially responsible for said participants' decision to enter the field of education. Kim went on to describe an early white savior mindset that her environment had impressed upon her, a need to 'reach' others without an understanding of the power differential between them, after which she matriculated at an Ivy League school (mine), which, as one might expect, 'didn't help.'

And now this is where the particular position of California as a centerpiece of popular culture comes into play. Racism as 'bad-but-distant' is undergirded by what its various industries produce, from the tech industry to Hollywood and everything in between. Cann (2013) referred to certain *white savior* movies – *wherein a virtuous white character ventures into a community of people of color and helps to improve their lives* – as part of what she called a 'public pedagogy' that everyone learns from, and that public pedagogy would be significantly weaker if it weren't for California. (And hey, now you understand the whole book title, finally!) The most populous American state holds a unique global position – it educates the world incorrectly while educating its own residents just as poorly about the reality around them.

Reality

'When I was 11', a colleague named Petra Star told me when I spoke to her. 'I entered the juvenile justice system because I had trauma. Once I entered the juvenile justice system I was pretty much the only white person there. And so in terms of language and diversity, a different experience, and then also I got a mental health incarceration sort of thing. And then sent to a boarding school, which is not a boarding school, but more like a "troubled teen" sort of thing. It's called the troubled teen industry. Basically, it's where they send mostly white kids instead of sending them to prison. So there's like a stretch, where like a sorting that takes place right? Like, white lady gets mental health care, all the kids that I was in the juvenile justice system with, they all got – even though they had the same behavior as me, the same issues, the same background, the same trauma – got sent into prison, usually. So that was a big awakening.'

Petra grew up in lots of places and moved around frequently, both within and outside of California, but in her description of her upbringing, she was raised in a similar location to the woman, Kim, I spoke to for my dissertation, where there were children of color *around*, but they'd been redlined into different parts of the county.

Now, a pause to define a few things for unfamiliar and/or international readers. First, as she described in her narrative, the 'troubled teen' industry, which has recently come under well-deserved fire, is indeed a series of largely unregulated 'institutions' where parents send their children to be scared into better behavior. From a study by a scholar and former resident in a 'troubled teen' center named Jamie Mater (2022):

> Over half of the participants had attended wilderness programs, and experiences varied from very negative (as recounted by most) to very positive (as recounted by a few). One person explained a common intake experience: 'They made me strip completely naked and cough and squat in front of two staff. I'd never been naked in front of anyone. I was 14.' Other participants recounted being taught 'self-hatred,' being 'treated like animals,' and going 'three weeks [without] wash[ing] our bodies' in the wilderness programs they attended. Positive experiences reported by participants were attributed to supportive staff and program philosophies encouraging self-love and acceptance. One person believed 'wilderness saved [their] life.' However, even those with more positive experiences recalled witnessing harm inflicted by staff on peers, staff automatically distrusting them, and having their progress negated once they left.

So that's bad, we can all agree, right? But I provide these details to show both the differences from and similarities to the American prison system, which Petra pointed out was usually where her peers were sent. She endured traumatic experiences at her 'boarding school', but unlike traditional incarceration, there is much less professional and financial consequence to having attended one of these 'schools'. In other words, as hard as these 'schools' are on their 'students', no one is going to hesitate to hire you just because they find out you've been through this. That hardly makes it 'worth' the pain, but this divergent experience is an example of how white children, particularly on the West Coast – *many troubled teen institutions are located in adjacent, sparsely populated states such as Nevada, Utah, Idaho and Montana* – are not inherently given up on, even if their attempts to 'save' them cause all sorts of additional distress to the children involved.

I also wanted to point out the concept of 'redlining', which many of you will be familiar with, but for the uninitiated, realtors and real estate developers quite literally drew red lines on maps of urban areas, isolating certain communities and thereby contributing to financial underinvestment, particularly in areas with large Black populations (Cornell Legal Information Institute, 2024). It's now technically illegal, but these communities continue to struggle, and Petra's point was that while she lived near these communities, it was clear that there was a dividing line between her experience and theirs.

A colleague and friend, Benji Woods, reflected on his experience as a language teacher in California when we spoke. He's mostly worked in adult and/or higher education contexts, and works in a part of the state that is, similarly, seen as an aspirational from the outside. His comments recalled something that Dr. Weaver told me back in the UK chapter about the way adult language learners are babied. As he explained:

> I think they're typically saying ... 'If you want to live in California forever, like this is what's going to happen,' and so whether that's a good thing or a bad thing or right thing or wrong thing, I'm not totally sure, but, but I think that tends to be the approach and then, you know, the thing that I see as a problem with the way that you know our teachers view students is you have to do a lot of training to get them out of the mindset that these are not intelligent people, right, like because they don't speak English or don't speak English well. A lot of the teachers here, when they're when they're doing activities and things they'll pull in like children's pictures and children's books and things that kind of appeal, I kind of hate these things, but on 'teachers pay teachers' [*a website where teachers ask for donations from other teachers*] they have those kinds of like cutesy art pictures and then they bring those into adult classes and you're like, 'These are adults. We need to talk to them on an adult level.' So I think there's a little bit of infantilizing on some levels, not always, but I do see some of it and it's like, maybe we should try talking to these people like they're adults instead of like they're children.... When I studied [an East Asian language], we did some kids things that were culturally related, and they helped me understand parts of culture, but we didn't read children's books you know, and we weren't kind of talked to like baby teachers or anything like that. I don't teach true beginners or very low levels either. And so I have an advantage to not really be in that world. Because you're like, 'Well, am I simplifying? Or am I infantilizing?'

You may be reading his struggle with these practices and wondering how this reifies racism, but as has been mentioned before, language skills – *particularly skills in a dominant colonial language* – have been used as a proxy for both sophistication and intelligence, and accordingly, be it in the UK or in California, adults become children. This also ties back into the earlier points about white saviors and public pedagogy, because if you can help a 'child' become an 'adult', you've given them a gift that will benefit them as they seek to flourish in your home context, thereby additionally implying that your identity is aspirational. I hope that argument wasn't too much of a stretch – I'm saying that, in this case and in other contexts as well, teachers are taught that helping adult learners of color improve their English will make them more societally palatable, even if race is rarely if ever discussed as a part of this equation.

The contrast between the racism in California and the more overt kind that the world considers 'true' racism can be summarized in two stories Petra told me, the first about her time working in Texas – *which isn't quite The South, but it works for these purposes* – and then an experience she had on the West Coast.

Describing an interaction with her supervisor in Texas, she told me the following:

> She had called me in her office and was like, 'You're doing really well at this campus [of a community college system]. So one campus was a wealthy white area, and the other campus was predominantly working class and people of color. And she was like, 'Wow, you're so brave. It must be so hard working there. I prefer working where the smart kids are.' And I was like, 'What do you mean by that? What's the difference?' And then she used eventually the word, 'the darkies' or something like that, like I have never heard that word. [A circa-19th century racial slur, for the record.]

In contrast, when teaching in California:

> I predominantly tutored 'the scholarship kids,' they didn't say, 'the kids who are different race,' they call them 'the scholarship kids' and, 'Oh, it must be really hard to work with those kids because they have behavioral issues and they're not as smart.' And so it was like the exact same thing but they never said the words, and then it was couched in this pity, like *the Blind Side* coach lady like, saving these kids. These kids are just as smart. You treat them like crap. And they deal with the racism from the other kids all day long.

The Blind Side is perhaps one of the most egregious examples of California-produced public white savior pedagogy, in which the wife of a high school (American) football coach teaches a Black student – *portrayed as barely able to speak or communicate* – how to use his massive body to play the sport more effectively and rescues him from poverty. The real athlete it's based on eventually played professionally. Great! Except it turns out the coach and his wife profited massively off the story and he never saw a dime from a movie that made hundreds of millions of dollars (Fletcher, 2023). But when that's what you're learning about the intelligence level of students of color, it's no wonder infantilization and negative stereotypes abound, be it from a supposed lack of language skill or behavior 'worthy' of incarceration.

What Needs to Happen

In a way I feel as though California is a 21st century version of what the UK used to be. And frankly what the United States used to be, too. Colonialism isn't dead, but it has a different, seemingly friendlier face, and it looks a bit like the movies we send around the world to burnish our image. Soft cultural power is far easier to maintain than literal land possession, and a lot cheaper, too. Public pedagogies are hard to fight because they're challenging to pin down, and the only real solution is to create counter-pedagogies, like the work I try to put forth, but, although I thank you for reading this, I'm never going to be as popular as *The Blind Side*. And though there are poorly sourced books and articles out there, they really don't fact-check mass popular culture, certainly not in the age of social media. So if there's any of the contexts about which I may have the least hope for its behavior to change, it might actually be California, because self-examination does not a blockbuster make.

I'll let Petra have the last word:

> Racism is like a monster that has so many heads and it just morphs and changes and it gets squirrely when you confront them or when you like, try and make them talk about something, they do this weird *Matrix*-style like move and the language they use around it is so opaque. If you say 'white supremacy,' they get weird about it. And they want to talk about something else.

I don't see the head that produces much of our public pedagogy being chopped off anytime soon.

6 Trying to 'Nice' It Away
The Midwest

Background

I wrote the introduction before the 2024 American presidential election, and I'm writing this after the results. Suffice it to say, my point that the Midwest would determine the winner was proven correct. I bring that up just to underline the idea that this region of the United States, while not the most powerful culturally like California, or the most powerfully financially like the Mid-Atlantic (from Washington, D.C., to Boston, inclusive of New York), is perhaps the most 'American' part of America, for better or (mostly) worse. It's not necessarily where most of us live, but it might be where most of us live inside of our heads.

Even its name is quintessentially American. Think about it. In literal geographic terms, what we call the 'Midwest' is actually better described as the 'Middle East' of the contiguous United States, which is a brief joke in the movie *Anchorman*, but is not without accuracy. The boundaries of the region vary depending on who you speak to, but, culturally at least, you could find yourself in the 'Midwest' anywhere from Western New York state to Missouri, or even Kansas, a range of more than 1,000 miles. Now, that's not a particularly huge range given there have been previous chapters on countries as large as Canada, but I do think zeroing in on the Midwest is instructive for the points I'm trying to make, as the perceptions of the region are perhaps the most direct contrast to the racism most around the world associate with the American South. Simply put, the Midwest is known for being 'nice' – *similarly to Canada* – but its past and present belie this reputation, and indeed, as mentioned in the introduction, the region was suffused with 'sundown towns' that contributed to its current relative lack of diversity.

Here are some relative metrics, sourced from Sander (2020):

> Our concept of the Midwest – of so-called 'Middle America' – remains strikingly whitewashed: one of white grandmothers making white bread, white farmers milking white cows – the overly nice, casserole-baking, country-living Midwestern people that remind us of a simpler, more

'wholesome' America. But these stereotypes wash out a much more complicated and diverse reality – or at least, two realities that very much co-exist. It's true that much of the Midwest is indeed white and rural: only 10% of its population in 2017 was black while 81% was white. But dotting the vast pastoral landscape are a series of large- to mid-size cities, mostly post-industrial and blue collar with severe issues of depopulation, poverty and inequality. And these Midwestern cities tell a different story than the quiet countryside towns. For example, four of the ten cities in the nation with the highest percentage of African Americans are in the Midwest. In particular, 77.61% of Detroit, Michigan's population is black – and so is 76.48% of Gary, Indiana's, 54.10% of Flint, Michigan's, and 45.37% of St. Louis, Missouri's. And again we see the urban-rural divide. According to one count, seven of the twelve Midwestern states have a black population percentage that's less than half that of the nation's. The same report notes that of 1,055 Midwestern counties, almost two-thirds are over 95% white and more than half have a black population share of less than 1%. While 75% of the Midwest's white population lives in metropolitan areas, the same is true for 96% of the black population.

The question I will ask you to consider is, why do we perceive the Midwest this way, as a very white bloc, when in reality it's better described as an extremely bifurcated subsection of our country?

Perception

Sander uses a key phrase above – 'Middle America'. That 'middle' is doing a lot of work, and it's worth unpacking – *I just can't think of a better word, I'm sorry* – a bit. Yes, there's the superficial analysis that the midwest is in the geographic middle of the country, although that's not really true – what we call the 'Plains' states (e.g. Nebraska and Kansas and Oklahoma) are closer to the actual middle. Indeed, the Midwest is firmly in the Eastern half of the landmass. There's electoral politics, where many of the states determine the winners of presidential elections. I'm not going to bother analyzing the arbitrary nature of the United States electoral college but the point is, candidates almost always need to 'win over' the Midwest to win the White House. But 'Middle America' means more than either or both of those things, as it implies something 'in between'. The South, the West Coast, the Northeast, and all the micro-regions within, have distinct and in some ways relatively extreme stereotypes in describing them, whereas the Midwest might just be the image conjured when the 'American Dream' is invoked. Obviously there are people who aspire to the largesse of a Hollywood star or a New York financier, or those who'd prefer to 'live off the land' in more isolated parts of more rural states, but, within the – *say it again with me now* – master narrative of the American project, the Midwest is perhaps the *ne plus ultra* of the image we as a nation try to put forth. Or at least, the perception of the Midwest is how we'd like to be perceived, and what a median American life 'should be'.

There was a time when reality matched this perception more so than it does today, in that American industry really did emanate from Midwestern epicenters, including the faded fortunes of our manufacturing and mining. With those industries waning, many in the region have struggled to persist, and indeed the particularities of our elections have often hinged not just on Midwestern voters but specifically on who can convince them that they'll help them be restored to an illusory past glory. And hey, I don't necessarily blame people for wanting to find a stability they've lacked because of technological advancements and other deleterious effects of capitalism, though how they choose to express this dissatisfaction sure doesn't have (Midwestern) 'nice' results for many people around the country and world. You can find a lot more about all of these things in Joan C. Williams's book *White Working Class* (2017), which isn't *just* about the Midwest, but largely centers on the region and its residents' hopes to reach and maintain 'middle' class status, and the ways this has impacted their political behavior.

Now, that red-hatted political slogan you're probably thinking of is only a half-truth, because, as I mentioned before, the mid-20th century was indeed a boom time for the Midwest financially. But, as the title of Williams's book implies – *and she does cover this in the book* – it's the *white* working class that is oft-discussed as such a potent political force. The 'working class' part is important, especially given the region's economic struggles, but bad faith political actors have weaponized said whiteness as a wedge issue to take the blame off of the actual villains of the story and stoked racial animus among the group. However, my saying this implies that this is new, that the Midwest used to be an equitable panacea until the last few decades, yet as I wrote in the introduction, Loewen's book *Sundown Towns* (2005) was inspired by the fact that he, as a Midwesterner himself – *as I said, he was from Illinois* – was once shocked to learn just how deeply ingrained structural racism was into the region that had raised him.

Let's see what he had to say:

> I began my on-site research in Illinois, for the simple reason that I grew up there, in Decatur, in the center of the state. Coming of age in central Illinois, however, I never asked why the little towns clustered about my home city had no black residents. After all, I reasoned, some communities are not on major highways, rivers, or rail lines; are not near African American population concentrations; and have not offered much in the way of employment. Probably they never attracted African American residents. I had no idea that almost all all-white towns and

counties in Illinois were all-white on purpose. The idea that intentional sundown towns were everywhere in America,or at least everywhere in the Midwest, hit me between the eyes two years into this research – on October 12, 2001. That evening I was the headliner at the Decatur Writers Conference. It was an interesting homecoming, because at the end of my address, I mentioned my ongoing research on sundown towns and invited those who knew something about the subject to come forward and talk with me. In response, a throng of people streamed to the front to tell me about sundown towns they knew of in central Illinois. Moweaqua (2000 population 1,923, 0 African Americans) was all-white on purpose, two people said. Nearby Assumption (1,261, 0 African Americans) was also a sundown town, except for its orphanage, Kemmerer Village, and the few African American children there often had a hard time in the Assumption school because of their color. An Illinoisian who 'grew up on a farm just west of Decatur and attended high school in Niantic,' a hamlet just west of Decatur (738, 0 African Americans), wrote later, 'I had always heard that it was against the law for blacks to stay in Niantic overnight. Supposedly, when the railroad section crew was in the area, they would have to pull the work train,with its sleeping quarters for the section hands, out on the main track for the night.' Another person confirmed the railroad story,and two others agreed separately that Niantic kept out black people, so I had to conclude that Niantic's population was all-white not because it was so small, but because African Americans were not permitted. Still others came down with information about De Land, Maroa, Mt.Zion, Pana, Villa Grove, and a dozen other nearby towns. (Loewen, 2005: 7–8)

What Loewen makes clear here and at many other points is something I want to triple underline. The South was obviously where most slavery occurred in the country, and its history of racist violence is well-documented. But sundown towns – ag*ain, where Black residents had to leave by dusk lest they be attacked* – were rare in the South because so many of slavery's descendants remained close to where they'd been dragged, my own ancestors included up through my grandparents' migration North. Indeed, the South to this day has a very high Black population. Whereas so-called Middle America quietly kept segregation in place for so long that during his research – *in the 21st century, mind you* – there were still all-white towns. Suffice it to say that there can and is danger for people of color all over the United States, but, speaking for myself at least, there's no part of the country where the perception of warmth differs so greatly from the reality of entrenched exclusion, but in such a way that it has successfully been hidden and promoted as welcoming and convivial. We'll see what my interlocutors had to say shortly, about both this as well as language ideologies, but from where I sit, that really doesn't sound very 'nice'.

Reality

Of all the places I scoured my contacts – *and their contacts* – for interview subjects, the Midwest was the easiest place to find people willing to talk about. Part of that is that for my aforementioned dissertation, one of the people I eventually interviewed for this chapter took my course alongside several of her colleagues, all of whom work at a university in the Midwest. But I think there's something about the Midwest, especially for white educators and scholars who have access to social spaces I will always be excluded from, that makes them feel like sharing their opinions. So anyway there will be more voices in this chapter than any other.

Dr. Coretta Regis works at a school in a state that culturally straddles the South and Midwest, and she told me of why she felt it qualified as the latter. 'I think across the country', she told me, 'if you don't live in the South, people want to distance themselves from living in the South, a lot of white people especially. Everything says "Midwest proud" and stuff like that. So I feel like they try to discuss it as more of the Midwest so they are separating themselves from the South and the ideals of the South.' This certainly tracks with my preconceived notions.

She continued:

> It feels very 'Midwest Nice.' Where conversations that people might disagree about do not happen. It was just, 'be kind to thy neighbor' kind of thing, very Christianity forward in the sense that we all just love each other and, and that's fine. And that's all we need to do. And with any issue, you know, with LGBTQ+ issues, and with race, that's just kind of how it felt, where the people that were having these conversations were new faculty in these positions. A lot of us weren't even from around here. We were trying to get the lay of the land of how the university was grappling with whiteness, but that's not even a thing that was discussed. And then I think you're right in the last couple years, like in 2020, when folks realized they couldn't just 'nice' it away. Actually, people still very much tried to just 'be kind' racism away.

Unfortunately, you can't just pick up a jar of 'nice' at the store and use it as a racism exterminator. And in a way, as she explained, 'nice' can really be just a cloak to avoid reality.

> I think if you ask someone, 'Well, why do you want to be nice?' They would say some sort of like, 'I like being nice to other people because I want other people to feel good and whatever,' but it's really just making yourself look good, instead of being kind. Kind can make other people feel good. But when you're being nice, you're saving face, you don't want to show your cards too much. So you're just going to be surface-level nice and that is something that I feel interacting socially here a lot, that

it is just self-preservation. They just don't want to say the wrong thing. There's almost a fear there too. Especially talking about racism and like they hide behind being nice because they don't know what else to say.

My discussion with another professor in the Midwest, Dr. Natalie Andrews, reaffirmed what Dr. Regis posited about niceness and fear. 'I always tell my students that when I'm in Ohio, I never know what anyone's thinking about me until I'm on the freeway', she said. 'Then I know when I'm in my car, and people are flipping me off, then I know what people think about me. The other time that I know is when they fill out end of semester surveys, and their names aren't going to be on the surveys. And I'm like, "Listen, if you have problems during the semester, I might be able to fix them." I'm actually a professor who cares that you're having problems during the semester that I'm doing something that isn't beneficial for your learning. And I'm actually not going to get angry at you.'

The more I had these conversations and pondered what they were saying, the more convinced I've become that Midwestern Nice – *and niceness in general* – is something of an attitudinal prison for both the people upholding it and those who are struggling to receive additional support in spite of its omnipresence.

Now, Dr. Andrews also works specifically in the language education space, and I wanted to hear how these topics overlapped. This won't surprise anyone from the United States really, but for anyone international familiar only with stereotypes of our country's racism, Dr. Andrews made it clear that she was absolutely never surprised a Black person or an immigrant would choose a southern city such as Atlanta over any of the places she's lived in and around the Midwest. The distance from the norm is particularly stark even if they may well smile in your face when you approach them. And given that it is her job to teach new and emerging teachers of English, who are thus responsible for engaging with these populations, she is well aware of the harm that can be – *and often is* – reproduced when people who hide their hostility all semester until the evaluations are then tasked with providing education to those who are very clearly seen as The Other in their communities. But they'd never say that out loud, of course.

One of the people I spoke to, Dr. Gillian Oscar – *look, I'm running out of fake names and am trying to make the real people chuckle* – was originally from the Midwest, but had spent the past several years working in UK academia, before having just moved back to this country, though she was still in the UK at the time of the interview. She certainly had a lot to say about the differences between the two, which will recall some of what was discussed in that previous chapter. Some of what she said reminded me distinctly of the false impression many have that US racial hierarchies were a Southern and not Midwestern phenomenon.

It's hard to convey to folks in the US that conversations about empire and colonialism in the UK and that involve the UK do not exist in public discourse here. They don't exist in schools. Students, when they learn British history, they go from Henry the 8th to World War One. And this is what my students have told me. They don't learn about empire. That's not part of the conversation. There aren't cultural opportunities to interact with the legacies of empire in a critical way, at least for white people. Like if you are a person of color in the UK, you are probably here because you were once colonized. And so that is a part of your daily life, but the people who have the decision making power in the country who are largely white don't have that exposure. And so, because of that, they don't have the structural familiarity to talk about these kinds of things. They don't have the vocabulary. In many cases, they live under the illusion that these things happened way way far in the past and no one alive had anything to do with them, which is not true.

So what I find interesting about this – *and I could have included it in the other chapter, but others said similar things and her Midwestern experience made it fit here* – is that it sounds exactly like what has been happening in the Midwest with regard to sundown towns, a living history that exists to this very day but that the regional master narrative – *indeed the master narrative of the entire country* – tells us was located Elsewhere. Insofar as the Midwest is part of the United States, she does consider the UK even further behind in its discourse on racism and language ideologies – *'living here has made me more patriotic than I've ever been, and I'm so annoyed by that', she said* – but as a subset of the larger national story, the Midwest represents an aspiration and finger firmly placed in front of ones lips to keep the facts from being found out.

Finally for this chapter, as I mentioned back at the start, Dr. Birch has recently moved from the Pacific Northwest to the Midwest, and was reflective about how the two places compared, especially given her own preconceived notions of each, since she's from New England originally. The coded racial language and the firm segregational boundaries arise in conversations she has with other parents, despite these all being extremely privileged academic types who, one might assume, would 'know better'. But I guess by this point in the book none of us should be making such assumptions.

> I think for me and for my husband, our goal is to not raise an asshole, right? And so part of that for us is exposing him to like what people in the city actually are like broadly construed, right? So like from a socio-economic perspective, from a racial perspective from all of these perspectives, I want my kid to grow up realizing that his perspective is not better in some way and thinking about how to not raise an asshole when you have like, I have this little blond haired blue eyed kid and I'm like, 'Oh

my gosh, what are we gonna do about this?' And that to me feels like our challenge for parenting. [Neighborhood in large midwestern city], where [the university where she works] is, is one of the few really socioeconomically diverse neighborhoods in the city. In that there's single family homes and apartment buildings and all sorts of public housing, all kind of coexisting in this neighborhood. It's also pretty racially diverse, which is nice. Especially for a [city] neighborhood where you do not see this kind of diversity. So for us, that feels like a great neighborhood to move to. But, you know, when when you're at a dinner party with 30-some people and you say you're moving from where we live in [other neighborhood] a very white, almost suburban neighborhood even though we're in the city, [university neighborhood], people are like, 'why would you want to do that? Aren't you worried?' But even *within* [university neighborhood], we're looking at a house that's like south of the dividing line between [adjoining areas]. And people are like, 'Oh, that's not a great neighborhood.' It is literally still [university's] campus. The law school is right there. What do you think is going to happen to us on this street? I think we'll be fine.

But I suppose, after decades of separation and silence, this is the stratification people are used to.

What Needs to Happen

For the first (but not last) time in this book, I'm asking readers to take action, because I don't think the stereotype of Midwestern Nice and everything it represents and prevents is going to change anytime soon without a direct response.

The image of the Midwest – *of 'Middle America' overall* – needs to be deliberately shattered. Not only because it's untrue and flattens real lives into two-dimensional creatures, but also because it works so well as a defense against raciolinguistic progress. If you know anything about America's ideals, about the American dream, I want YOU to ask yourself if it resembles what has been described in this chapter about the Midwest, and do whatever you yourself can do to challenge these concepts. American popular culture subverts these expectations often enough, but the master narrative remains in place. So, whether you are personally familiar with the Midwest or not, I ask readers to question what's in place, where it came from and why those stories are being told to you.

7 The 'Right' Kind of Spanish

Mexico

Background

It has definitely occurred to me that titling these chapters after entire countries, or even just regions of countries, feels a bit like proffering the idea that this is the definitive assessment of both racism and language in said context, even though, aside from the statistical citations I've offered, I'm mostly just sharing stories and opinions from people I trust. If it helps, then, you can change the titles in your head to 'a snapshot of how a certain subset of the populace, with time and inclination to ponder such things, considers race and language in said context'. I bring this up at the start of the Mexico chapter because we all well know the interesting place in which the country sits, directly beneath the United States and treated as scum by many of our politicians, a perfect example of Western (and white) xenophobia that also encapsulates racism, classism and linguistic ideologies. But for the actual people who live in the country, who number more than 125 million at last count (Mexican Census, 2020), the supposed non-American-ness – *and non-whiteness* – of the residents is far more complex and nuanced, not only because so many (white) Americans have chosen to move there in recent years, thereby gentrifying various areas and pricing the locals out of their homes (Arellano, 2022), but that's a topic for another day. No, I think that Mexico, though treated as a terrifying boogeyman of violence by right-wing neighbors to the north, is a pertinent example of a country where white supremacy has long been a factor, even if most of the country wouldn't be considered white were they to travel elsewhere. Mexicans are descended from both conquerors and conquered, the Indigenous populations scarcely better off than those mentioned in the chapters on Canada and Australia, yet rarely acknowledged when Americans speak of the reasons we should fear the country. Indeed, Mexico is the most populous Spanish-speaking country in the world, but that sentence also elides the fact that Spain was no more virtuous than the settlers who stole the land to their north; despite how Americans and others may view users of Spanish, it is no less of a colonial language than English. Accordingly, regardless of actual skin tone, few classify individuals from the country of Spain as anything other than 'white', or at least 'European' more so than 'people of color', whereas, Mexicans suffer a different fate in the United States, even though plenty of them can be racialized as white on a superficial level. Indeed, it is that conflict between superficial classification, the status of Spanish and other languages spoken in Mexico as liminally powerful, and their proximity to our gravitational pull that made it compelling to me to have a conversation about the country. Hopefully once we get to that section it will prove to have been of value.

And, for the record, I'm not really going to do the racial percentages this time – Mexico defines its people quite differently, and I point you toward many such books and studies accordingly. Suffice it to say, though, that the national image of Mexico, while outwardly pluralistic, flattens some of the nuances found among the people, and the hierarchies we've seen in other countries are no less present there, even if they have a slightly different flavor.

Perception

Ciudad Juárez and Cancún.

For the most superficial of external observers, these two places stand in for the public pedagogy informing many of what the vast, varied country of Mexico 'is'. With the former, you have a metropolis that directly abuts the state of Texas and represents the exaggerated, xenophobic, and frankly racist fear that US figures use to stoke anger and vitriol of our southern neighbors. Discussions of Juárez drug cartels – *which certainly exist, but it's not as ubiquitous as our media would pretend* – dominate right-wing political agitprop, alongside 'migrant caravans', often misleadingly pictured with the implied threat of their impending 'invasion'. I shouldn't have to tell you why all of this is problematic, aside from it not exactly matching reality. We can't really play the same game with Canada given their relative demographics, so when you slap brown faces onto the TV screen, it's a whole lot easier to evoke panic from people who are under no real threat.

At the same time, though, Americans love to have a party in Mexico. Cancún is probably just the most well-known of the country's tourist destinations – *and yes, I've been there myself; I am not presenting myself as morally superior here* – but you could use any of the many resort-centric areas to illustrate this point I'm making, that we flatten the country into a hotbed of rampant crime while being happy to have it as a place to visit whenever we see fit. At least in the way the United States conceives of the place, Mexico is beneath us in both a literal and figurative sense, and raciolinguistic ideologies are absolutely a part of that ugly equation.

Case in point: one of those very right-wing ideologues who rails against said crime was caught fleeing to Cancún during a weather emergency in his home state of Texas (Livingston, 2021). Mexico is as convenient a vacation spot as it is a scapegoat for issues we ourselves are responsible for. Now, I make that statement there, but, unfortunately, I can only present a broader argument rather than an acute one about current conditions. When I say 'we' are responsible, I do mean that global colonial powers – *as well as the perception of an easier life* – contribute greatly to poor conditions in Central and South America. But the specific reason why each individual or family travels to the United States is hard to pin down because it requires the sort of longitudinal study that is built by precise, hard-won data that is absolutely not coming out of the current situation. What I do feel comfortable saying, then, is that, as I wrote in my first book, the way we speak of the danger coming from below is little more than a 'dark projection' (Gerald, 2022a) of our worst impulses and not reflective of the way most who venture to this country actually behave.

I cannot speak for people from the UK and the rest of the Commonwealth, but by and large, Americans have a thimble-deep understanding of who Mexicans actually are. We think they all speak Spanish – *though some of us think they speak 'Mexican, by which they do not mean a Mexican variety of Spanish* – and that their entire cuisine is similar to what you might find in our 'Tex-Mex' restaurants on this side of the border. We think of deserts and beaches and violent cities, but some of Mexico's cities are considerably more modern that what you'll find in the States, especially when it comes to their actual investment in public goods such as transportation (Mexico City Tourism board, 2024). In fact, let's compare Mexico City and Dallas, Texas, which is a bit of an unfair fight as you'll see, but given the way Texas treats migrants that journey through Mexico, it's an instructive comparison.

Here's what Mexico City has to say for itself (citation same as above):

> Traffic can still slow you up and it's recommended that you look into the Metro, get used to it, and learn to use it for the majority of your daily trips. It's affordable, reliable, and usually quite a bit faster than most other kinds of transit...
>
> The Mexico City Integrated Mobility Card [is] your ticket to a rapidly expanding list of transit methods that will get you all around Mexico City...
>
> Mexico City Metro [is] your best bet for nearly all travel within the city...
>
> The Metrobus System runs along seven dedicated lines within the city and costs (with the same smartcard as the Metro system) just six pesos. For many neighborhoods, and many points of interest, the Metrobus may be your best option. If you see the distinctive red Metrobuses moving near your hotel, you may very well want to investigate which line it corresponds to, and be that much more mobile.

Great. This may all seem like minutia, but I really would rather focus on this than include the awful, racist statements our media has uncritically promoted about the country. Indeed, when searching for a verifiable source about migration, most of the results were biased and hateful, and I prefer not to include said things in my writing if I can help it.

So what about Dallas then?

Dallas is all suburban sprawl and highways. There is nominally a public transportation system called DART, but most people drive, and drive exclusively. The city encourages people to walk, but given its massive spread, this is often infeasible. I say this not to pick on Dallas per se – *there are many American cities like this, and it is far from the worst I've visited in this respect* – but to point out that we often do a worse job of taking care of our own residents than the government of Mexico does, despite the stereotypes and scapegoating. To cite an old quote from the former mayor of Bogota, Colombia, Gustavo Pietro, 'A developed country is not a place where the poor have cars. It's where the rich use public transportation.' This is but one example, but I ask of you, between the United States and Mexico, which is the developed country?

Reality

Jackie is a teacher who lives in Arizona with Mexican heritage. I found her angle interesting because unless she told you – *or you knew her full name* – you would have perceived her as white, just like my friend from Canada. To put it bluntly, she looks more like Cate Blanchett than Salma Hayek. I've always been fascinated by people who could access white spaces while having a different perspective, and admittedly part of the reason I keep writing these books about whiteness is because I can never, by definition, access a fully white space and see what it's like, not that that would be fun for me, but you get my point. So anyway, here is some of what Jackie told me:

> In Mexico, it's kind of interesting, because there's lots of people who look like me, but I think in Arizona in particular, the image of what a Hispanic person looks like is very specific, and so as a white passing person, people don't really see like … they get really comfortable being a little racist around me. Arizona is a pretty historically [conservative] state, and so I've heard a lot of interesting negative connotation, interesting words regarding race used around me because white people think that they're safe to say that stuff around me, and so I think my experience is unique in the sense that I have heard a lot of people say things that they probably would not have said if they had seen me and immediately known that I'm Hispanic.

Her experiences tracks with mine, not with regard to Mexico of course but because, though I am visibly identifiable as Black, I have spent so much time in 'elite' white spaces that people assume that I'm a Safe Black Person. It's not the same as being seen as white, so they definitely don't relax as much as they otherwise might – *but again, I'm just assuming* – but I'm still someone that, for many years, white peers felt way too comfortable sharing their true opinions with. Maybe it's good for my scholarly career that I was privy to their honesty, but it was still hard to take, and I've spent the last decade-plus trying to ensure that no one thinks I'm someone they can convince to co-sign their racism.

Similar to praise for Black people being well-spoken, Jackie has also experienced the confluence of racism and linguistic ideologies because she speaks Spanish, and this has added to her understanding of the way people mash language, race and intelligence together.

> When people find out that I speak Spanish, they get really excited and think that it's really cool. And I've had a lot of people who, especially like in school settings and things like that, who will tell Hispanic people, 'speak English at school' and things like that. But then they'll hear me speaking Spanish, and they'll go, 'Oh, that's so cool. Where did you learn that?' So it's kind of been interesting to see that, like, my second language is cool because I'm white, but learning English as a second language is seen as lower in the social hierarchy. I experienced that as well at work with kids, especially who are learning English as a second language. That's kind of seen as an annoyance. It's seen as, you know, that student is lesser than or that that student is more difficult to work with, when the reality is that it is a really big deal for them to know two languages as well and to be learning as they are learning content in school. And so I had a lot of experiences where I'm like, 'Hey, why is my Spanish cool but theirs isn't? Or why do you tell them to stop speaking Spanish at school?' But it's fine when I do it.

I've brought up popular culture many times in this book, not just because it's an interest of mine but also because it is the message that cultures share with the world about their society. Most people will not visit a given place, so their understanding is going to be shaped by what is globally propagated. In speaking of Mexican media, Jackie concurred with the fair-skinned nature of many Mexican public personalities. 'All of the popular actors are all still people that are light-skinned', she told me. 'So, you know, you still kind of see the same things, the desirable traits are still, you know, like that. That's what is considered beautiful. And the racism there is not necessarily the same as here, where the judgment is coming from the othering of people who are outsiders. So it's more visual, it's more like what you see and what you perceive to be desirable traits.'

This is a key point here, and it ties directly into the overall perceptions I am hoping to challenge with this work. Obviously racism is partially a visual thing in the United States (and everywhere else), but the way racism is publicly taught to the masses suggests that the United States *only* and *disproportionately* uses visual cues to assess racial categorization. What I mean is, although American racism is pervasive and systemic, simplifying it to skin color is both inaccurate and dangerous, for several reasons. First, other countries are in some senses even more focused on actual color than we are when determining racial hierarchies, and second, because it makes it all that much harder to have racism taken seriously when slurs and skin tone aren't involved. What Jackie is describing about Mexico isn't good by any stretch, but if it's at all possible for us to dispense with the related ideas that the United States is the *most* focused on skin color, and that skin color is the primary determining factor in racism overall, we would all be much better off.

> I have siblings that look a lot more like they're like my mom's side of the family, I favor my bio dad a lot more, and he's, I mean, all kinds of white European. My mom's side of the family is Mexican and Spanish, and so my experiences are definitely different because you don't look at me and see like a Hispanic person. I don't look like my siblings. I don't have the same features. One of my brothers is more light skinned and has green eyes, but his bone structure and his hair and things like that takes after more of the Hispanic side. So, you know, it is definitely, it is definitely a thing ... I did have something that I thought, so regionally in Mexico, there are certain traits that are favored in different places. And so the way that people talk about people from different places, when they're like, talking about people in Oaxaca, like, 'oh, they're kind of dark,' or, 'they dress kind of funny,' or whatever. And then different regions have different accents, and so they talk about the way that people talk, the way that people pronounce certain words.

I personally find it interesting that in a place like Mexico where race is thought of differently than it is in the United States, their adjacency alongside their having a very different history with chattel slavery, none of our American hierarchies are any less present, but filtered more through region and language. In a way, this is somewhat more similar to how racism operated before the slave trade, where people were categorized according to regions (again, see Painter, 2011 for more) and superficial differences, but there wasn't nearly the level of racial identity work that has recently been undertaken and shared with the world.

I say all this not to shame Mexico for being, sadly, human, and not too different from many of the other places from which I found people to interview, but more to point out that that the shape of racism changes, and the angles shift, but the core desire to rank people based upon their identities remains central to the organization of society, and the more we touch on places where English isn't the primary language, the more

I believe we'll see that linguistic ideologies factor into that hierarchization. This is not to say that raciolinguistic ideologies are absent from the United States of course but more that because we have such an extensive body of racial discourse that focuses on *race qua race*, as much as certain people would like to deny it, it is understood that racism is a factor in this country. I am certain the people discriminated against for their race in each of these countries are well aware of what I'm saying here, but I do think, given the United States' prominence on the global stage, there really is a paucity of understanding regarding how much more global this sinister story really is. Ultimately, Mexico is no less of a colonized country than the United States is, but their relationship to their Northern bullies helps their own racism fly under the radar, much to the detriment of the people who might otherwise be seen more equally.

What Needs to Happen

I do think this is sort of the United States' fault, to some extent. By 'this', I mean the way Mexico has raciolinguistically organized itself. I don't mean to imply that the country lacks an independent mind and spirit or that we control them, much as our politicians seem to wish we could, but that we are inextricably linked, both compared and contrasted at all times. I do have slightly more faith in our southern neighbors to challenge their colonialist hierarchies than I do in the portions of the United States I'm touching on in this book, because both visual and regional distinctions are highly salient to most. The subtle aspects of racism that show up throughout this book certainly do exist in Mexico, as does coded language to hide its harshest aspects, but the impression I get, and, like this whole book it's obviously just one man's opinion, is that this is the sort of context where to call out oppression that falls along racial lines as being racist despite it rarely mentioning racial identity – *even if it does mention skin color* – might be dismissed. The looming specter of the hostile American xenophobia and racism then becomes a double burden for the oppressed within the country, for the entire country can rightfully claim that our rhetoric treats them as inferior, thereby lowering the urgency for those on the bottom of the social structure to receive the support they need. It's a mess, basically, and unlike a lot of these chapters, in which I have been arguing that the United States is hardly the only locus of racism on earth, I do think we have had a significant harmful impact on the Mexicans who can't silently move through all-white spaces without being noticed.

'When you hear people categorizing others, or when you get the urge to categorize people', Jackie told me,

> we need to develop more of an awareness of questioning where that comes from…. Where are these stereotypes or these ideas coming from,

and why were they created, and how are they perpetuating our divide as humans, right? How are we continuing to judge each other or fight each other, and how is that keeping us from, I mean, not to get like conspiracy theory about it, but when we're all pitted against each other, we're not really questioning the people who benefit from it the most, right? And I think that that can apply to pretty much anywhere that you go.

'The history is so different everywhere you go', she concluded. 'But the intention is the same.'

8 EFL on a Rampage
South Korea and Japan

Background

As I said way back in the introduction, it might be mildly discomfiting to see those two countries mashed together here. It's the only time in this book I'll be combining more than one entire country, and I don't think I need to review their extensive history of conflict to explain why people in each place might want to insist upon their separation. But this book isn't merely about different cultures broadly, and I absolutely would – *and will* – delineate the two in some ways. However, I'm writing about race, whiteness and language here, specifically language education when at all possible, and, for reasons I find dispiriting, the two actually do overlap on this subject.

Unlike some of these recent chapters, I've actually lived in South Korea – *I visited Japan briefly while I was there* – and my decision to go there was somewhat arbitrary. Once it became clear to me that I wasn't going to get a stable job after college because I'd petulantly rejected the financial services path chosen by many of my classmates, the internet informed me that, with a bachelor's degree, I could easily be hired to teach English overseas, which is how this whole faction of my career began. I'll get into the issues with how the hiring of fully unqualified teachers is problematic for both said teachers and the students – *in fact, a sizeable portion of my first book is about this very topic* – but I wasn't in any place to complain about this, both because I didn't actually know this was the case, and also because I wasn't mature enough to care when I was 21.

The only qualifications I had before moving halfway around the world was a one-week class I took from a disreputable company that no longer exists where they 'trained' us in teaching, which for them essentially meant how to write a lesson plan, along with a five-minute language instruction demo. I think I did fairly well, but it's not as if the people who did poorly weren't allowed to graduate, and the class paid for itself because it raised my salary in Korea by a few hundred dollars a month.

But it was actually hard to choose between Korea and Japan. I was fairly ignorant of both cultures, though much more so of Korea, and both countries had strikingly similar government-run programs at the time, with nearly identical acronyms. In Japan you had the J(apan) E(xchange and) T(eaching) program(me), and in Korea, you had the E(nglish) P(rogram) I(n) K(orea). Both programs would fly out massive cohorts of mostly unqualified teachers, provide accommodation and some level of support in adjusting, and install you in a local public school. I could lie and tell you there was some sophisticated reason why I chose Korea, but I essentially flipped a coin, and the internet told me that Korean would be easier to learn, which it is, but I still failed to do so.

So in a sense, this chapter is really about what feels like the epicenter of the unqualified EFL teacher paradigm, two extremely developed and modern countries that still hire people mostly for their nationality – *and, implicitly, race* – rather than their skillsets, and the possible impacts of this system that is sadly far too similar in two neighboring countries that will rightfully tell you they're not the same.

Perception

The article I'm about to cite isn't exclusively about East Asia, but it applies quite accurately to the environment there, and the manifestation of the English as a Foreign Language industry there. Ruecker and Ives (2015) review online advertisements for overseas teaching jobs, and described their analysis as follows:

> Criteria for the ideal ELT candidate are often implied through imagery rather than stated explicitly. The images of teachers on the homepage suggest that the ideal teacher is a young, white, enthusiastic native speaker of English coming from a predominantly White country where English is the official language. ELT professionals from countries other than those listed, and those for whom English is not a native language, are not addressed. The overall message is clear. There are plenty of opportunities in this industry for young, typically inexperienced, recent college graduates from Western nations interested in short-term adventure. Nonnative-English-speaking teachers from countries outside of the approved list, regardless of qualifications, need not apply. (2015: 2)

We need not rehash the decades old debate about so-called native speakers and why they're not inherently more effective than those who learned the language later. Even if it would be difficult to prove beyond a reasonable doubt that 'native speakers' are inherently worse, they're certainly not innately more effective just based on their nationality. And of course, native speaker status is subtly – *or not-so-subtly* – used as a proxy for race. I mentioned many chapters ago that I was told that schools in the city I lived in (Daegu) saw a white, female Canadian as the ideal teaching candidate, and I remember exiting a subway station during my time there and seeing a giant advertisement featuring a picture of a 23-year-old woman I knew, who had all of a few months' experience at the time. To quote Ruecker and Ives above, 'the overall message is clear', and reinforced by both the types of advertisements the scholars analyzed, pitched toward potential teachers, as well as the advertisements within the countries, pitched toward parents who desperately want their children to stand out in their English skills.

But does it help? I mean, my own perspective aside, wouldn't it all be validated if the way standardized US English was prized actually helped these students? Wouldn't the ends justify the means, in other words? Well.

There isn't much evidence that the exams assessing standardized English in East Asia actually demonstrate improved skill (Kim *et al.*, 2019a). So ultimately, a better score isn't necessarily indicative of linguistic development, but is a comparative status symbol, more representative of parents' expenditures and potential future income than of expertise, even as the learners know how rarely they're likely to make use of the language from day to day. As Kim *et al.* (2019b: 103) wrote in the article cited above, 'jobseekers objectify their learning results, and submit them into the neoliberal job market, waiting to exchange it with material profit. In the course of such score-building competition, the English tests turn into the ends in themselves and spawn stress and demotivation unconducive to learning.' Obviously, you spend years forced to consume standardized English, you'll be more familiar with it on at least a superficial level, but it has no bearing on whether or not they enjoy using the language, and in fact puts many off of it.

On top of all this, then, there's the fact that even if they succeed, such as it were, and attain top-notch test scores, and maybe even move to an English-dominant country for their studies or career, because they are classified as non-native, they will never really escape the stranglehold that raciolinguistic ideologies have on the way they are perceived. As Kim *et al.* (2019b: 79–80) wrote, 'In addition to experiencing fatigue because of having to work in a language that is not their native one, nonnative speakers also experienced fatigue from constantly monitoring their own actions and thinking about how their actions will be interpreted or evaluated by others'.

Now, you might point out that this isn't unique to South Korea and Japan, and, sure. The EFL industry is global. But these are two particular examples of countries that are not classified as 'developing' – *a condescending term I only use for convenience here* – but that count very few white individuals among its residents that are neither teachers nor members of the Western military, which its own dark story we don't have time to analyze. Accordingly, my argument is that, with the possible addition of Taiwan, these are some of the most extreme examples of the power that English has over contexts in which I don't believe it should be relevant. There's no real reason why English there should be any different than my having learned French in high school, is my point, but it's a core part of the curriculum, a narrow sliver of the language that exists only in tests and textbooks yet has a massive impact on students' futures.

Finally, there's the impact this has on the teachers themselves. For the white teachers, though plenty commit to the work and choose to improve, there is little to no incentive to progress beyond the status with which you arrived, which often leaves these individuals with the long-term choice to remain in East Asia for perpetuity or struggle career-wise if they return home, like many of my friends did – American (and Canadian, etc.) employers have many issues, but they are correct in believing that there's little professional growth inherent to being an EFL teacher in East Asia, so it's relatively meaningless on a CV, a fun curiosity that never qualified me for more than part-time contract positions. And then, for the teachers who aren't white, particularly those who are Black, there's how we're seen while we're doing the job, where students, unfamiliar with anything beyond stereotypes, assume we're from Africa or that all cities we live in are rife with violence (Charles, 2019). In a stunning moment of honesty, my employers at the high school where I was placed even told me they'd only considered hiring me because I had an Ivy League degree, which they implied made it possible to brag about someone who was Black.

So, this EFL system, such as it is, is a perfect encapsulation of the raciolinguistic ideologies and hierarchies at play across this book, though in a much more structural sense than the interpersonal dynamics that have occupied most of the other chapters. I thought it would be beneficial to see how a context in which whiteness is mostly and quite literally foreign is still impacted by the hierarchies that all of us cling to, regardless of how physically distant we may seem to be from the source of said ideas.

Reality

'I think you said you mentioned possibly doing Korea and Japan', Dr. Maya Edwards told me, 'and I would say go for it. Because I think if you're thinking about at least the way race is understood I don't think those are separate conversations or histories.'

This validation from a friend of Korean descent was a big part of why I proceeded with this combined chapter, so I did want to include it here to demonstrate I wasn't making up the justification. But the meat of what she said was actually surprising to me, as you may well see.

She continued her thoughts accordingly:

[My family and I] would get a lot of like, really surprised responses to the fact that we would speak English, but then the second time we went back was post 2012 K-pop craze, you know, *Gangnam Style* had already come out and suddenly America knows where Korea is and decides to go and visit you know, whatever, the whole nine, but then the thing is is we still didn't go to the city. So we were still in the countryside, still lots of surprised reactions, a lot of people asked if I was from Russia, like specifically right off the bat. 'Where did you come from, are you from Russia, what are you doing here? Why are you speaking Korean?' There was this kind of fun moment when we went to a restaurant. We did not realize how fancy it was when we showed up there, but the chef came out and he's like, 'I'm so honored by your presence in my restaurant. I'm so impressed with how well you've learned Korean and after only being here for a short time,' and I'm like, 'I didn't say how long I was here, but okay.' So I would say that's kind of the general vibe and I have friends who live in Japan and my partner's Japanese and I think it's kind of a similar concept where in some places that are less touristy, they still think of themselves as like, very homogenous, racially, linguistically, and so curiosity, that sort of thing could just be leading them to think that.

A few notes here. First, my older son – *six by the time you read this* – loves the Psy song *Gangnam Style*, and the popular dance quickly reached the point where it was just something children do rather than an authentic representation of culture, which is interesting given the song is satirizing Korean conspicuous consumption and debt. Second, this response came after I asked about how she was seen, given she has the interesting position as being clearly racialized as Asian in the United States but seen as foreign by Koreans because she's of mixed heritage (and Russia is nearby, hence the assumptions). I experienced similar shock at my extremely limited Korean – *hers is fluent* – when I tried to practice the language while I lived there, and in truth the main reason I never learned Korean beyond the alphabet and the basics is that everyone responded to me in English when I tried to practice. Like the EFL industry in general there, I had no incentive to make progress. So I didn't.

Going back to the original question of whether it's appropriate to combine the two places, Dr. Edwards had this to say.

'It's interesting, right?' she started,

Because Korean and Japanese are both housed in the same 'East Asian Studies' home. What does that mean? Like, what does that mean? And if you actually dig into it with Korea, and Japan's history, like it is a racial or racialized historical conflict and that sort of thing, and they did for a long time see themselves as distinct and all of that is just like politics and history. But if you just change the context and come back to the US, suddenly, it's all basically the same, right? Let's just put them in the same department and let's kind of treat them both the same.

In a way I am guilty of this in this chapter, which is a difficult tightrope to walk. But I make this choice because the global raciolinguistic system performs the same task, flattening different groups and places into the same identities despite their historical differences. I wanted to consider how EFL had squashed these countries into one entity, to the point that my consideration about where to work was purely financial, and one in which I didn't think twice about the potential differences in culture. In other words, these countries are not the same, but in a Western, English-dominant perspective, they are mushed into one East Asian context. This entire writing project, really, is a meta-conversation about the way that ideologies of both race and language contort reality, and as such, I contend that this combination makes sense in continuing the narrative at hand.

> I almost feel like conversations about race with folks I know who are from Korea. I almost feel like what I imagined conversations about race were like when I was a kid in the 90s with white people. You know what I mean, where it's kind of like this weird, 'we're all Korean. We're all multicultural. And anyone should be able to belong,' and like, they don't quite say 'I don't see race,' because they'll recognize diversity and that sort of thing. But then, the stereotypes still come out, the microaggressions, whatever people want to call them. I know that for a lot of South Asian, like, and other minority immigrant groups, they still experience racism and discrimination, but the discourse is that 'we're multicultural,' and, 'everyone is welcome and everyone could be Korean,' but like, socially, that stuff doesn't actually always play out.

It's interesting to note her comparison of Korean racial discourse to 1990s United States discussions of the same topic. It all feels a bit like time-dilation, the concept wherein time works differently for objects moving at significantly different speeds, usually on an astronomical scale, but I think it fits the topic here. For all of our past, present and future misdeeds on racism in the United States, I think it might be reasonable to posit that our position as a growing, powerful nation in the late 18th century, and the fact that white landownership was categorized as true citizenship in our official documentation, means that, I don't want to use a positive word, but although racism is older than the United States, the version we all currently contend with was, in some ways, crystallized by us, especially given our involvement in chattel slavery alongside the reality that, as mentioned in previous chapters, this occurred primarily within our borders, unlike the UK and other European nations, though there are exceptions to this, of course. All of this is to say, for better or worse, we've had a very long time, relatively speaking, to sit with the version of racism we thus propagated, and though that absolutely doesn't mean we're free from the curse, it does mean that, if the color-evasiveness

Dr. Edwards describes is rampant in countries such as South Korea and Japan, there is something of a time-dilation effect occurring in the places we've influenced culturally.

Additionally, her mention of South Asia refers to the fact that, like many places, there is an ethnic group outside of the majority that is tasked with many of the least glamorous jobs in the country. Although Dr. Edwards referred to South Asia, the migrants to South Korea come from places such as The Philippines, Thailand, Vietnam and other such countries (Ramos, 2024). And in Japan, as was sadly the case in most places, it was migrant workers from other parts of Asia forced to bear the brunt of the COVID pandemic, performing manual labor with little pay and little protection (Clean Clothes Campaign, 2020). I expect, due to the way that Western perspectives flatten Asia into just a few regions, people consider this economic and linguistic hierarchization separate from racism, but my own experience helps me understand how this is no different from the way anti-Blackness works, even if it's not Black individuals being discussed at all times. In both South Korea and when I visited Japan, locals would try to guess where I was from before I spoke to them. Once I spoke, they assumed I was either African or American – *and usually a soldier* – but beforehand, they saw unidentified Brown skin and shouted countries at me, not with hostility but just curiosity. I usually received Vietnam, Thailand, Philippines and Bangladesh as guesses, all of which are pretty funny given what I look like, but in retrospect, it seems more like they were seeing whether or not I was a migrant stepping out of his station in society, sitting next to them at the sauna or on the subway. The fact is, the colors themselves are almost the least important part of racism, especially when white is rarely one of them. The point is the societal rankings, and that practice remains strong in the places we in the west read about in what we've decided to classify as East Asian Studies.

What Needs to Happen

I mean, this is the English teaching industry in a nutshell, is it not? This environment is the apotheosis of what English has wrought around the world. These students are forced to learn a version of English starting at age five – *if their parents don't pay for them to begin even earlier* – and only a very small percentage of them will ever need to use the language beyond the basics. The way almost everyone (including them) has to study math, they need to study English, and there is a maelstrom of malevolent forces holding this system in place. Unlike some of the other contexts described, which almost necessarily are linked to the United States or UK, South Korea and Japan do not need us. If we removed the economic pressure that English applies, they might happily thrive without us, but that pressure persists, and so there remain thousands of mostly white faces imported to serve as cultural and linguistic ambassadors more so than effective instructors.

I will give them credit, though. I've spoken about public pedagogy several times in these pages, and the popular culture from both countries in question does a far better job at attempting to challenge hegemony. Even that now-toddler-approved *Gangnam Style* is deeply critical of what is valued by the public, but, just like we tend to accept our own harmful public pedagogy uncritically, most of us just hear a fun melody and dance without looking up the lyrics because, as was the case for me when I lived there, there's little incentive to learn these languages, despite how much they're pressured to learn ours. And even now, when people ask me, despite my years of being critical of the hiring of unqualified teachers, I still tell interested parties it's a valuable experience to have had, which makes me a part of the problem all the same. So, they're trying, is my point, even if they're probably stuck in our EFL quagmire for the foreseeable future. I wish them the best of luck.

9 Learning Colonialism
Algeria

Background

As you might be able to gather by now, there's no way I'm going to be able to cover every corner of Earth, and not even every aspect of a given context, as this is qualitative, narrative-based work. That's intentional, as I believe the entirety of whiteness and linguistic ideologies is essentially a fictional story we've all been told and that we ascribe to to varying degrees, but the point is, you can see each chapter as a stand-in for a certain type of context. For the Pacific Northwest, you can think about places you've been told are particularly progressive but harbor an ignorance it would rather not admit to. For the Midwest, a veneer of niceness as a cover for a history of malice. For South Korea and Japan, the epitome of the English as a Foreign Language industry as it exists – *and persists* – in 'developed' countries far from where English is a fact of daily life. And so on, for the chapters that follow this one. But now we come to a chapter on Algeria, a region I've never come anywhere close to visiting, and while that didn't particularly bother me when pondering racism in a predominantly white setting such as Australia, I do want to be careful in how I approach this here.

As an entry point, though, I will mention that, geographically, the closest I've ever been to North Africa – *I've been to Southern Africa* – is the South of France, which is actually appropriate given the history of the two nations. In fact, in my more progressive French classes, my teachers and professors attempted to be honest about the 'colonial relationship' between the two countries, which is definitely a euphemism. So, although this is about Algeria, like the rest of this book, it's really a story about Europe and, to a lesser extent, the United States and all we've wrought across the globe.

Speaking of the United States, people from Algeria have now awkwardly slotted into a 'new' racial category in the census – *though who knows if it'll persist to the 2030 version* – called 'MENA', an acronym for 'Middle Eastern or North African'. Now, we can quibble with mushing those two regions together the same way 'Asian or Pacific Islander' comprises a comically large area both geographically and culturally, but there was a legitimate reason for the change – they were previously considered 'white'. As Hassanein (2024) wrote:

> Iyman Hamad, a Palestinian American public health graduate student at Wayne State University in Detroit, had to search online to figure out which race or ethnicity box she should check at the doctor's office and on school forms. And Itedal Shalabi, who runs an Arab American family services center in the Chicago area and is also Palestinian, said misinformation and hesitancy about COVID-19 vaccines were rampant in her community. Because Arab Americans were considered to be white in the absence of a category for them, county funding for outreach in minority communities was delayed, probably causing avoidable deaths, she said.

This wasn't just a random oversight, of course, and I would look to the brilliant work of scholars such as Dr. Neda Maghbouleh, who chronicled the Persian community's journey into and out of the majoritized racial category in her book *The Limits of Whiteness* (2017). Extremely long story short, there was a reason some within the community argued for inclusion, but as the news article cited above shows, this has obscured their reality, in both the United States and elsewhere.

Perception

This portion will touch on concepts that have recurred throughout this work, namely, colonialism and certainly race and language, but this is the first time it's been worth considering another axis of identity: religion.

Not literally everyone in Algeria – *and especially not everyone under the 'MENA' umbrella* – follows the same faith, but it is for all intents and purposes a fully Muslim country, as over 99% of those who follow a religion consider themselves Muslim according to the Arab Barometer (2019). It should be noted here that a growing segment of the population does not consider themselves religious, driven by the country's youth, as is the case in many places, but this isn't really about hard facts – it's about perception. And as such we need to talk about anti-Muslim (or anti-Islamic) racism.

Now, I know what you might be thinking if you're unfamiliar with the term – religion and race aren't the same thing, so that must be something of a misnomer. We already have *Islamophobia*, right? And if it's about their nationality and/or language, we already have *xenophobia*. Scholars on the subject acknowledge this, but the concept holds value nonetheless. Bringing nationality, religion and race together in one fell swoop, Fekete (2004) wrote the following about what she conceptualizes as a new paradigm of racism:

It is xeno in form in that it is directed against foreigners irrespective of colour; it is racism in substance in that it bears all the hallmarks of demonisation and exclusion of the old racism – and the mechanisms that set that foreign-ness in situ are legal and structural and institutional. What appears to have happened post-September 11, though, is that the parameters of that institutionalised xeno-racism – anti-foreignness – have been expanded to include minority ethnic communities that have been settled in Europe for decades – simply because they are Muslim. Since Islam now represents 'threat' to Europe, its Muslim residents, even though they are citizens, even though they may be European born, are caught up in the ever-expanding loop of xeno-racism. They do not merely threaten Europe as the 'enemy within' in the war on terror, their adherence to Islamic norms and values threatens the notion of European-ness itself. (2004: 4)

Not that there were any Algerians involved in the September 11 attacks, but to people without a nuanced understanding of the people in question, none of that matters. What Fekete and others make clear is that the racism that targets religious communities, Muslims in this case, follows the exact same patterns as the 'old school' racism of exclusion and subjugation based on group membership. I won't include them here, but there are plenty of slurs used to describe these individuals, one of which even includes the 'n word' that remains considered the apotheosis of offensive diction in English.

I bring up this violent intersection to frame how the people are seen from the outside, by the countries in which I'm sure that most of you live. Just as white Americans came to fear slaves and use any instance of their attempts to seek freedom as justification for furthering their racist project, Algerians have fought against colonialism for as long as they've been occupied, but in the 21st century, there's an additional global 'danger' to liberation sought by people who are both members of the Islamic faith as well as phenotypically seen as what we now call MENA.

Make no mistake, though; language has been a vital aspect of Algerians' fight for freedom – upon their independence from France, language planning was a central part of their path forward (Benrabah, 2005). In this way, their anti-colonial resistance has resembled that of many newly independent nations. However, because of that day in September, the wars that followed and the displacement and emigration to predominantly white countries that occurred subsequently, any fight they put forth now is much scarier to those who might have otherwise ignored their desire to establish their own identity. Fekete (2004: 4) continued from the previous excerpt:

Since Islam now represents 'threat' to Europe, its Muslim residents, even though they are citizens, even though they may be European born, are caught up in the ever-expanding loop of xeno-racism. They do not merely threaten Europe as the 'enemy within' in the war on terror, their adherence to Islamic norms and values threatens the notion of Europeanness itself. Under the guise of patriotism, a wholesale anti-Islamic racism has been unleashed which itself threatens to destroy the fabric of the multicultural society.

So even though most Americans themselves don't spend very much time differentiating between MENA countries and cultures, because it was something that happened in New York that helped crystallize the form of racism visited upon these people, I did think it worthwhile to touch on their role in all this. It is clear, however, that Europe is a primary driver of these sentiments.

All of this is without even having acknowledged that people classified as MENA look very different from one another and even perceive the group they ostensibly belong to differently vis-à-vis race. As Maghbouleh (again!) *et al.* (2022: 6) explained,

> The perceived relationship between MENA individuals and skin color is complex. Whites associated a medium skin tone with MENA categorization. MENA respondents, on the other hand, viewed both light and medium skin colors as more typical MENA traits. These different understandings of who represents MENAs suggest that significant portions of the MENA population may not be read as such by others, which could have significant consequences for street-level discrimination. At the same time, the fact that Whites associate MENAs with a darker skin color underscores the fact that they seem to understand MENAs as a group with a non-White phenotype.

In other words, even though plenty of members of the group consider themselves as either part of or adjacent to lighter skin tones, I would argue that anti-Muslim racism has helped ensure that, to racially majoritized individuals, they are firmly classified as 'other' and lesser.

Of the many reasons why all this is plainly harmful is the fact that when racism and attendant stereotypes coalesce around a group, their actual existence is flattened into but one dimension. It's good that we can discuss how best to challenge these oppressive structures, but it doesn't give us much insight into how racism operates within the country, and while I can't say it's necessarily *worse* than the racism emanating off of white Europeans and Americans, it also makes it harder for people within the country experiencing the impact of raciolinguistic ideologies to be heard. So I hope that as you read through the conversation that follows, you will learn about race, language and Algeria from someone who doesn't think they're all the same.

Reality

Dr. Yasmine Saidi is a scholar who works out of the UK but was born and raised in Algeria. When we started our conversation, she provided useful context about her experiences of having relocated to one of the other countries we discussed earlier in the book, but added the angle of religion that we are just now tiptoeing into.

As she told me:

> The whole discussion around race and ethnicity in the Global North gets dismissed as soon as there is another identity that is minoritized for the white person and therefore when there are discussions around discrimination, you will find white women who are teachers, my colleagues, saying, 'Oh, I can relate to that. I can't fully relate to your experience as a person of color or religious minority, in my case being an immigrant as well.' So there are all these elements of my identity that have informed the discriminatory experience that I would be narrating or sharing with my colleagues who are white women, then the phrase I would be comforted with is I can't relate to what you're experiencing. However, as a woman, when I was working in a predominantly male environment, I experienced this and harassment and this and that, and therefore somehow, you know, especially white women can relate to the experience of being minorities who have been discriminated against, but the elements of race would never be part of the discussion.

If I can clarify, essentially, her white female colleagues have sought to bond with her over shared experiences of gender-based oppression but are not particularly willing to listen or consider how her additional minoritizations have complicated her work and life in the UK. In a way, this desire to connect can actually push minoritized peers farther away, as we can tell not only how different our experiences are but also how far our peers are from having a clear understanding of it.

Digging into Algeria itself and what I mentioned in the previous section about challenging racism within a historically oppressed and colonized country, she shared that my suspicion was accurate, and that accusations of racism often have cold water thrown on them immediately. What I wasn't necessarily expecting was that the majority religion itself would be used to dismiss said accusations of racism, but I suppose I shouldn't have been surprised given how often Christianity has been perverted to the same ends around the world.

> When I talked to my cousins based in Paris, in France, being you know, second generation immigrants, and I asked whether they speak about whiteness and privilege and things like that, in France, Gen Z does, and that's because of the exposure they have to social media. If we travel a

bit south to the north of Africa, and in the case of my country, Algeria, racism is very present, but the ability to be present as the aftermath of colonialism but also present *because of* (emphasis mine) colonialism. But people are not necessarily aware that they are reproducing colonialist hegemony or reproducing colonialist discourses and behaviors and practices because they also justify their racism the same way it is justified in the Global North to be honest, because the system of harm and oppression functions in similar ways. So if we were to talk about interracial racism, it exists in Algeria, but then it gets covered up with verses from the Quran that says we are all equal. And then whenever you dare to challenge somebody and say, 'Oh, this is not okay. What you're saying is racist,' it's like, 'we're not racist. I'm not racist. Our religion is not racist. Our religion teaches us that we're all equal, and we should be respecting everyone equally.' But in practice, that's not the case.

So there's quite a lot in that excerpt there and I'd like to go through it in detail. We see a lot of what we've already heard from other interviewees in previous chapters, and a few things that are brand new. There is one key phrase I want to zero in on that might as well be this book's hidden subtitle – *though there's probably a bunch of those by now* – and I want to know if you can figure out what I'm referring to before I tell you in the next sentence. 'The system of harm and oppression functions in similar ways.' (Did you get it?) People are simply not that different from one another, and country borders are mostly imaginary – *aside from the oceans and such* – and based upon colonialist violence and/or arbitrary political decisions. Cultures are different, as well as languages and races and religions, but it's still all one master narrative of justified hierarchies, and ultimately that's all that racism is. And, by now, it makes so much 'sense' to us, that it produces something of a teleological bias, or the mistaken assumption of causality.

Allow me to explain: since you were not the one who stole a country or created the system that subjugates a particular group – *even if you are benefiting from this subjugation, whether you are willing to acknowledge this or not* – until you do the work to study and question these systems, the relative lack of power of particular populations is all you've known, and it is what you are accustomed to. Therefore, especially if you are among the more powerful in your society, your power must be righteous, thereby making the other groups' lack of powerful similarly correct. And because it would be disorienting to believe that races or genders or what have you are stratified by pure chance, then many of us – including me and you – ascribe to the stories that 'explain' why it's alright for this to be the way of things. If you are a person of faith, then, your belief system has to explain the way of the world, so, as Dr. Saidi mentions, you will find some phrase or some teaching that, essentially, keeps the world spinning. That might have been too theoretical for some readers, but I think the point is sound.

Dr. Saidi presented a grave reality when it comes to the impact of racism within the country, especially as it pertains to people with darker skin than hers.

> People who are of Black Heritage or are racialized as Black, are called Africans by Algerians themselves. So the fact that there is this dissociation from Africanness, by the Algerians themselves speaks a lot about the heritage of colonialism because Algeria historically was considered an extension of France. And therefore, although the Arabs were labeled Arabs or Indigenous, regardless of their ethnicity, they were all put in one same umbrella. As soon as they start talking about the rest of the continent, then whoever is Black is African, which means as a light-skinned African myself, I wouldn't be referred to as African, which is scary for me, but speaks very, very loudly about how the intricacies of racism and harm are rooted and implemented in a post-colonial context. So how does the racism look like for a person who is Black in a country like Algeria, then translates through language, and then terminologies and terms and objectives? With a student population who comes from Sub-Saharan Africa, from countries like Tanzania, Kenya, Nigeria, who will travel to the north of the continent to study, they would be considered 'violent,' 'savages,' 'ill-behaved,' all terms that you would find in English, you would find them in Arabic and in French to reduce a whole population of Black students for example, to their to the primitiveness of the colonial language, you know? So if a group of international students coming in from African countries that are predominantly Black resist the institution or organize a strike or try to protest the situations that they are put in and the conditions they study and live in? Then they would be treated and addressed or described as being 'uncivilized,' terms that were used on us Algerians by the colonizer? So it's still happening today.

Remember a few pages ago when I was warning about how these structures obscure oppression within cultures we stereotype from afar? I don't say this to shame Algerians for being anti-Black – *it's not good, but it's hardly unique to them* – but I do want this example to help us understand, first, that the Global South is hardly immune to the same harmful ideologies that have propagated from the Global North, and second, that racism is immensely powerful, because plenty of those students she mentioned are, themselves, Muslim, and would, one might assume, be seen as brethren. Yet the fictional stories we've told ourselves about who is beneath us make it harder for societies to find the equality they profess to believe it. And unfortunately, those stories have proliferated even into places that have nominally thrown off the shackles of colonialism.

Dr. Saidi concluded accordingly: 'If a student who is coming from a country that is predominantly Black, again, I've cited a few example [countries], I'm happy for you to pick one. It doesn't matter because they would be considered all the same afterwards. They are the Africans anyway, they are essentially reduced, dehumanized, and considered just the same in terms of behavior, so that individuality is denied.'

What Needs to Happen

This one might make me the saddest of all. Not that every former colony is the same, but there are literally hundreds of countries you could say have had the same experience as Algeria, being owned by a European (or, later, American) empire and finding its way to freedom. There are countries that quite literally are still yoked to their former owners financially, which is unfortunate, and I have no expectation that that practice will conclude any time soon, but what concerns me here is the ideological influence that European powers and the structures they created continue to exert over the places they nominally no longer own. That might read as infantilizing of Algeria and similar places, and I am by no means saying they do not have their own independent thought, but if the people who ascend to power and influence in the vacuum of post-colonial transition do not wholeheartedly reject not just the legal ties to their former controllers but also these underlying thought processes, then the marginalized within their borders will continue to struggle apace. The particular horror of anti-Muslim racism in the 21st century adds to the difficulty in this case, but that's just what we can refer to now – there's always going to be a New Racism that applies to different groups of people.

I am not claiming there will come a time when we can point to a country that lacks hierarchies. Humans are far too complex and difficult to manage to arrive at such a utopia. But if we in the Global North are going to continue to influence other countries in harmful ways, then I believe it is also our responsibility to put forth a better ideological example, even if the sub-Saharan students in Algeria have no idea that their treatment is a part of the global master narrative that insists on persisting.

10 Trapped in the Sunken Place

New England

Background

Ah, New England. The slightly colder region that has always been adjacent to where I've lived. For those unaware, New England is essentially every state northeast of New York City until you get to Canada, though some parts of New York State itself qualify. That means it's Vermont, New Hampshire, Maine, Massachusetts, Rhode Island and Connecticut. Though I went to one of the exceptions (Princeton), most of the universities that comprise the so-called Ivy League are located within the region, meaning that we have classified this area as the intellectual hub of the nation, for better or worse. And one thing I learned when I moved to the city I now live in – *Yonkers, New York* – is that, though this is seen as something of a suburb because it's adjacent to New York City and therefore much smaller, its population of more than 200,000 (US Census, 2024) would place it first among every single state in New England, with the exception of Massachusetts (because of Boston). This is the city population itself and not the metropolitan area, but Yonkers is part of NYC's metro, as is much of Western Connecticut, so those distinctions are muddy and not of much use. The point I am making is that it is an area of relatively small-population settlements, known for bucolic autumn weather and changing leaves. It is, of course, where the country first established colonies – *they landed in Virginia first, but the 'Mayflower' was in New England* – and is accordingly considered the oldest part of what we call the United States.

I don't really want to repeat myself from the other chapters about regions of this country, though. Is it seen as politically progressive, like the Pacific Northwest? Yes. Are people considered polite, even if less superficially 'nice' than the Midwest? Yes. Is it more racially homogeneous than you might have assumed? Yes, even though there are plenty of exceptions. But what I really thought was worth zeroing in on was ... money. New England is, overall, a relatively wealthy – *and expensive* – region of the country. Almost all of the states in New England are among the top 20 states (out of 50) in household median income, and the ones that aren't – *Maine and Vermont* – have a relatively lower cost of living (US Census,

2023). It's also a relatively educated region of the country, as there are many more top-tier schools in addition to the Ivy League that dot the area. Unlike household income, there are zero exceptions to the educational attainment statistics, as every single state in the region is top 20 for percentage of residents with undergraduate degrees (US Census, 2022).

What is my point in bringing all of this up? It's hardly the wealthiest or most educated region of the world, after all. But if the initial point of the book was to demonstrate that the public pedagogy of the American South being representative of racism writ large and American racism in particular, then surely the region that's about as far, ideologically, from the South as possible would be able to avoid the same behavior.

I think you already know what's going to happen next.

Perception

Chilly. That's the first word that comes to mind for me when I envision New England. Not just the autumn and winter temperatures – *it's 13 degrees Fahrenheit or negative 10 degrees Celsius as I write this from New York, and much of New England itself is far colder* – but the demeanor and the, for lack of a better word, vibe.

That's not a random thing to discuss, because, if all of these chapters are in some fashion a response to perceptions of racism based on the American South, then one thing you can say about that region is that it is absolutely perceived as warm. Similarly, the sweltering summer temperatures are a part of that, but the phrase 'Southern Hospitality' exists for a reason, and refers to the supposed warmth the residents show to one another in their interactions. This isn't about the South, so I won't go too much into it, but said warmth and the 'niceness' discussed with regard to the Midwest and Canada don't precisely have the same connotation. Think of hugs and physical contact (warmth) versus avoiding saying negative things (niceness). Obviously, both regions harbor racism in their own ways that runs counter to either warmth or niceness, with the South's being world-renowned and the Midwest covered earlier in the book. But both of these concepts stand in contrast to the chill of New England.

Readers from the UK who have visited the region may staunchly disagree, but New England, as you might gather from its name, is about as close to 'European' as the United States gets. It's the only part of the country that actually has something of a public transportation system that people frequently use, as mentioned the education levels are higher, and it is, obviously, the closest geographically – *although Maine is also the US state closest to mainland Africa, despite often being the whitest state in the country. Funny.*

Despite its reputation as relatively forward-thinking, many of the colonists who landed in – *and stole* – New England certainly had slaves, and, eventually, the region developed a healthy share of sundown towns just like the Midwest did. Indeed, there are municipalities adjacent to every major city in the region that until recently were entirely white, all of which was covered in the aforementioned book by Dr. Loewen.

So when I say 'chilly', I am talking about a demeanor and an attitude, something that visitors from other parts of the country point out when they visit. People from New York City and Boston themselves are often considered 'rude', which usually just means overly direct and impatient, but aside from these stereotypes, the best way I can describe New England is to return to our public pedagogy and the pop culture put forth about the area.

So let's talk about *Get Out*.

Get Out, if you are somehow unaware, is a 2017 movie that it is difficult to categorize in terms of its genre. It has elements of horror, comedy and drama, is probably best overall described as a thriller and is deeply, furiously satirical at its core. Written and directed by former sketch comedian Jordan Peele, the movie was a word-of-mouth sensation upon release, and has quickly attained a reputation as a classic, having won the Academy Award for Best Original Screenplay, a rare feat for a filmmaking debut, and still – *as of this writing* – the only instance of a Black artist receiving that award. Now, that's great and all, but why am I bringing it up?

Well, *Get Out* takes place in an unidentified region of New England – *supposedly a rural area of New York state, though it's never specified in the dialogue* – but every person of color watching the movie knew where it was set immediately – wherever the large, well-manicured family estate is, we know we're in Liberal White New England. The story follows a young, Black photographer named Chris who is invited to meet his white girlfriend's family for the first time. He's nervous but is repeatedly assured that they're progressive and accepting, and upon arrival he's greeted by the father, a surgeon, who makes awkward jokes, slips into African American Vernacular English – *'how long has this thang been going on?'* – and professes admiration for the recently concluded administration of Barack Obama. Now, look, Peele wrote the movie over several years and filmed it in 2016, but the fact that it came out mere weeks after (the first time) Donald Trump was inaugurated was not lost on audiences, even though it was a coincidence.

Anyway, though I could probably recite it from memory, I'm not going to recount the entire plot. Suffice it to say, there's something nefarious going on underneath the surface, and, spoiler alert, if you haven't seen the movie and would like to be surprised – *skip to the next paragraph!* – it turns out the family has a, um, side business abducting Black people and using their bodies as 'vessels' so that wealthy white individuals can experience what it's like to be married to a Black man, or 'gain' the supposed athletic skill of Black bodies, or, in Chris's case, understand what it's like to have his artistic talent, though he eventually figures out what's going on and escapes, barely. All of the 'reasons' why they need Black bodies for their bizarre fantasies are rooted in stereotypes about sexual prowess, athleticism and so forth, stereotypes as old as slavery and somehow not eradicated to this day. All of these stereotypes are on display during an extended sequence at a garden party, where Chris, as one of very few Black guests, is questioned by middle-aged or older white individuals about every single superficial assumption they've made about people who look like him. The film ends with a cathartic paroxysm of violence as Chris fights his way out of his fate, but the garden party is, to me and many others, the actual most terrifying part of the plot, because every single Black person I know who has spent time in New England has been at a party just like that one, and had those questions asked to them, and had to deflect and shrink away from the scrutiny. Thankfully I don't think anyone I know has been abducted and forced into being a vessel, but I guess I don't know for sure.

In the film's most striking and perhaps most impactful innovation, the Black individuals don't technically perish once they're abducted, but are instead hypnotized into what the family's mother, a psychiatrist, calls 'The Sunken Place', a terrifying void from which they can only watch as their bodies are used by the people who have paid to do so. The film has received plenty of academic analysis in the past eight years, but much of it has centered on this concept, a powerful metaphor for marginalization and unheard terror. When Chris is briefly sent to the Sunken Place, we see him screaming and trying to escape, and, as Allen (2023) points out, the movie isn't just saying that the structures of racism itself are a dark void of terror – the movie is specifically about white liberal racism, which is related to but distinct from the hood-wearing version many still boil the concept down to. Add New England's other details to this idea, the high level of education and income, and it's liberal, academic-inflected, wealthy racism that the movie is underlining for all to see who bothers to pay attention.

In other words, while it's certainly scary to have to run from racial terrorists, but in a context such as the movie's garden party, or an environment with individuals such as the family in the movie who profess to support people of color but ultimately just want to exploit them in perpetuity, because the racism everyone agrees upon is so overt – *and indeed this is the version still propagated via most, though not all, of our popular culture* – if you were to try and shine a light on the type of racism you'd find in New England, your screams may well go completely unheard, because no one is threatening to put you in chains. Before the events of the movie, Chris is nominally free, and conditionally accepted into white spaces. Very few residents of New England would support formal segregation in the present day, and would be happy to welcome exceptional individuals into their environments. But the half-hearted embrace New England provides is, indeed, a chilly one, and hardly one we can fully trust.

Reality

I spoke to Peter Crowley, a language teacher from New England, to seek his perspective as a lifelong resident of the area, and what he's heard and seen, especially as it has changed during his lifetime.

'So the schools I went to were predominantly white', he told me. 'And New Hampshire is a very white state. I had one Black classmate up to eighth grade and a handful in high school. I went to State College so it is a little bit more diverse but still largely pulling from New Hampshire residents and gradually, there's been extremely slow but a bit of migration both internally from neighboring states as well as where I'm currently working and in my role now. Manchester and some of the other cities, Nashua, Concord, less so, but Manchester in particular is a refugee resettlement hub. So there's a large population of Congolese ethnic groups.'

As I said a few pages ago, none of these cities are large. Manchester is the largest city in the state and has something close to 120,000 residents (US Census, 2024). UK readers will obviously notice its name being identical to that of a major British city, and you will find that all over New England – though sometimes, as with the name of the entire region, they add a 'new' in front of it (e.g. New York). Peter mentions Congolese refugees, and I mention the low population to point out that the few thousand refugees resettled in the region over the past decade might not have been very many in a massive city such as New York, but is enough to have a noticeable impact on the area's low levels of diversity – New Hampshire, Maine and Vermont enjoy dancing around each other to see which state can be the most homogenous as all three are more than 85% white (US Census, 2020). How (new) English of them! Inconveniently for my joke, West Virginia also has a similar percentage, but the point stands.

Now, those few thousand refugees may continue to change the state's demographics, but, as you may well expect, they are often shunted into a small number of areas that agree to house them, thereby recreating residential segregation reminiscent of the past, as pointed out by New Hampshire Public Radio (2021). Of course, these refugees also speak languages other than English, bringing us to our normal status quo of racial and linguistic marginalization being compounded.

Peter explained how these ideologies have arisen in his career.

> In my previous jobs prior to working with the current position that I do with the refugee population, I was in higher ed. And we were working with international students, who were largely wealthy, who were from countries with big economies, China, Saudi Arabia. And, you know, the kinds of

pushback that those students experience is very different from the kinds of pushback that students I'm working with now are going to experience and the ways that I would kind of try to leverage what power and influence I had within my department. So where in higher ed, a lot of the students who were attending the program, in the way that the program was run, they were sort of siloed within their program until they were considered to have enough English to integrate into their majors. That created an impression that was pretty widespread on a lot of the faculty that these students are, their English isn't up to par. [My colleagues were] not ready to be active listeners, to work at comprehending someone who might have an accent from their first language or to read, you know, accented writing and to do the effort. They're largely looking at things from a deficit model. And the only bits of headway I really made were in areas where there's already some receptiveness to that because they're adjacent to the kind of work I was doing with the English department, the Writing Center, tutoring, support services, linguistics. People in the sciences, people in the business school really were like, *I don't know if these people are a good fit for our programs.*

So this brings in the elements of class and how that can somewhat but not entirely blunt the impact of raciolinguistic ideologies. The wealthier non-refugee students are certainly treated better, but their language and identities still other them in the eyes of certain instructors. And again, this is supposedly the most enlightened part of the country.

Peter did mention that racial slurs are not completely absent from New Hampshire, but he provided an example of, essentially, someone who he assumed would 'know better' engaging in reflex uploading of linguistic hierarchies that exacerbate racial stratification.

The more genteel version of it can be the, *are they going to be able to keep up with this kind of work,* or you know, professional work or academic work or whatever. One example I have that was a subtle bit coming from someone that I really would have hoped would be more with it than he was was a professor who's now retired but like, his progressive bonafides were very legit, like he went to jail with Noam Chomsky once for participating in a protest. And in a meeting about how the non-ESL portions of the English department should consider working with multilingual writers, he said, '*Oh, I have a student, she's a senior,*' and in the same sentence, he said, you know, '*her writing is beautiful and intelligent. And also, I have to mark it down because of the grammar errors.*' Like, what? You don't have to! You are literally the third most powerful person in the department. No one is going to tell you that you have to do this. Like, you know, just say good writing is good writing.

Now, if that student tried to point out that this was unfair, it would probably be ignored given the professor's status. Though, more upsettingly, she may well have agreed with his assessment, as said deficit mindset is pumped into all these students, to the point where, many times in my own career, I've worked with learners who were competent and otherwise confident but still certain that they were 'bad at English'. Peter mentioned students such as this requesting help with their accents and how he'd try to demonstrate that he, like everyone else, said things in a way that sounded different, in his case a New Hampshire accent, but it's difficult to break ideological structures that are far older than we are.

Peter concluded this anecdote accordingly:

The thing that really stood out was he was saying not just that he liked the ideas, but that he liked the writing, like that he liked the imagery, and this was someone who was making interesting creative writing choices in their second language and he still couldn't get over his own hang-ups. About things he perceived as being more important than that.

And if someone like this is determined to uphold the raciolinguistic status quo, then what hope is there for the people who are trying to be heard as they scream from the Sunken Place?

What Needs to Happen

We need our bubble burst. I do say 'we' here because although I technically live just west of the region, it's so closely tied to New York City that I do feel conditionally a part of New England, especially given how often we visit relatives in Connecticut and Rhode Island. As the semi-digression into *Get Out* demonstrates, though, I have never felt particularly comfortable in New England when not in the homes of loved ones, and I think that there is a condescension emanating from the residents about their relative value compared to the rest of the country. We do tend to consistently vote against politicians like the ones currently in power, and imply we'd rather be a part of Canada or Western Europe than the United States, and in this respect, New England is fairly similar to the previous – *and upcoming* – chapters on these locations, looking down on the boorish, overt racism that we consider ourselves to be better than. Whether it's our income or our educational attainment or our voting patterns, or some mixture thereof, New England thinks it's superior to the rest of the country, and if you think you're the best, what impetus do you have to change?

This superiority complex is not just wrong-headed, though – it's also implicitly racist. The states with the opposite metrics regarding income and education are largely in that very region the world saddles with the 'racism crown', the American South, and surely there is plenty of oppression leading to those statistics. One might argue, then, that if people of color, and particularly Black people and those who speak other languages, wanted to find more health, wealth and opportunity, they ought to move to an area like New England. This is what happened during the aforementioned *Great Migration*, before which these areas – *and other cities such as Chicago* – were even less diverse, but here we are, stumbling toward the middle of the 21st century, and New England has conspicuously failed to evolve, walling off its minoritized groups when they have been allowed some form of access. Yes, it's expensive to move and thus not everyone can, but the point I am making, somewhat elliptically, is that if New England was a place we wanted to be, where we felt comfortable and welcomed, we would be there. So until New England gets off its high horse about the way it feels to someone who isn't from a majoritized group, it's going to continue to frolic in its fall foliage while failing to find a way to be the equitable place it thinks it already is.

11 The Goodest Country

Finland

Background

I read a book once called *The Smartest Kids in the World*, by author Amanda Ripley (2013). This was back when I wasn't nearly as well-versed in literature about racism and equity, and I was deeply impressed. In a way, this book had a somewhat similar structure to the one you're reading, as it was an international comparison between different contexts. These days, I would raise an eyebrow immediately at such a title – *how does one objectively quantify and compare intelligence, especially at a group level?* – but back then, about a decade ago, I was consuming every pop science education book I could get my hands on as I prepared to apply for and start my doctoral studies.

Anyway, part of this book is about the Finnish education system and how it purportedly outpaces that of the United States. In the book, an American student has a much improved experience after moving there, and as an author whose books are based on stories, I can't sit here and try to claim that this girl's experience isn't predictive, as it's not meant to be, but it is certainly well-crafted and evocative.

I've certainly never been any closer to Finland than, I guess, the few hours I spent in Amsterdam on a train from London to Paris, and what little I know about it comes from its idealization during my early adulthood. Particularly during the – *now clearly naively* – optimistic attitude of the first Obama term, the American media spent a considerable amount of time discussing how we could be more like places such as Finland and, amusingly given their placement earlier in the book, South Korea and Japan. I think to a lot of people, myself included, there was little understanding of the fact that Finland is not actually considered a part of Scandinavia, and that its history is quite distinct from its Norwegian and Swedish neighbors, but to many, I think that it was lumped in with those two countries and placed on an educational pedestal.

One thing that's certainly true is that very few outside of the region would meet a person from Finland and racialize them as something other than white. Many are at least somewhat aware of the struggles that

Irish-American and Italian-Americans once had being accepted as a part of the racially majoritized, but Finland? FINLAND? No way, right? We'll talk about it.

At the same time, though, I choose Finland as an example of a place that, from the outside, is likely perceived as even more racially homogenous than the UK or Canada or New England, and as such, as I learned more about hierarchies and oppression, I began to see the way that these countries were idealized as somewhat simplistic given what I perceived to being their lack of issues with race and racism among their residents. I felt the same way about South Korea and Japan until I spent time in East Asia – that these 'smartest' countries might have reached this position because they didn't have to deal with issues Americans or Western European countries have to contend with in educating their populace.

Finland in particular has often landed at the very top of the 'world's happiest countries' lists (e.g. Navarre, 2024), ranking highly on gender equity, paid family leave, and, yes, educational attainment, among other factors. And hey, like I said, I've never been there, so from my vantage point, it has always just seemed like a wintry paradise. And hey, for the first time in this book, maybe my assumptions will have been proven correct.

Just kidding.

(And for the record – it's not untrue that Finland is relatively homogenous both racially and linguistically, with over 90% of the country both identifying as ethnically Finnish and speaking Finnish as their first language – in fact the country doesn't even officially track ethnicity and uses language as a proxy, which is ... interesting (National Center on Education and the Economy, 2021). That doesn't mean that these same hierarchies don't exist, though.)

Perception

So I want to ask your opinion, though. Outside of the context of their own country, and, if you met one in your country of residence, would you classify Finns as white? Just think about the answer.

Finland is a fairly interesting example to plumb deeper into the concept of racialization, and the process thereof. Indeed, though the name of this book was originally a cheeky pun, I do think there are, and always have been since the broader idea was solidified, 'shades' of white and whiteness, and in both this chapter and the following one, I believe it's valuable to explore how two of these shades have interacted with their position within the umbrella.

Gonzalez-Sobrino and Goss (2019) provided a detailed description of the value of considering 'racialization' as a process instead of just race as a static fact, especially given it is not a biological truth. I've spoken to this a few times in the book – *considering the newly created category of*

'MENA' and what that meant for people whose identities were being reformed around them – but the impact of this process for people that most of us wouldn't even think twice about classifying as white is interesting in the context of this work.

The authors wrote the following:

> The importance and uniqueness of the experiences of black people, as well as the continued forms of antiblack discrimination, still holds true. Yet, there is a profound need to explore the experiences of new (and old) racial and ethnic groups that transgress the colour binary, even as they are informed by its historical and social structural dominance. While scholars increasingly bring data and analysis to the study of race and ethnicity that is irreducible to the black–white binary, special attention should be paid to the theories and concepts used by these scholars. Accordingly, the racialization thesis has a special appeal for scholars that move beyond and through the black–white binary. That is, the racialization approach affords the theoretical tools to understand both macro- and micro-level processes of group formation and exactly how these processes function – that is, their mechanisms. Many published works on racialization either focus on the racial meanings attached to actions, places, or organizations, or the attachment of these meanings to a group of people. Either approach serves as a robust theoretical tool for understanding both structural racial inequality and everyday interactional discrimination. Racialization has a particular usefulness to study race in international and transnational contexts. The use of the concept and the focus on the mechanisms of racialization help scholars understand how, for example, national groups become understood as racial groups through immigration or how racial meanings shift over time and space. Racialization affords social scientists the theoretical manoeuvres to understand race and power beyond a particular social context and social time. (2019: 506–507)

I mentioned just above that within Finland, there is no official distinction between a national group, a linguistic group and a racial group. Government data holds that there is what you speak, which is usually also where you come from, and that's simply who you are. Many of the questions this book hopes to address are related to the way groups are envisioned by those who are outside of them, particularly that of races. To put it another way, while race is not a biological fact, it is a structural reality, yet it is a unique one that only exists in contrast. You could say that about other aspects of identity too such as gender or religion, but our modern form of race is so closely tied to separation that it will be a long time before we can make this claim with a straight face. You can be a Muslim, say, and it technically means you're not a Christian, but your faith can exist far more independently of other belief systems; similarly, what it says on your passport may only exist because of colonialism or arbitrary borders and provide you (or deny you) certain rights, but you can be classified as a resident of one country without it specifically conjuring distance from another. Obviously I am over-simplifying here – *ask someone from Busan if being Korean* doesn't *mean they're not Japanese* – but I am attempting to build towards the point that to be within a race is to be outside of, above, below and/or in opposition to other races. To many of us reading this, Finns are white, and potentially part of racial oppression, but to many Finns, they are merely Finns, only somewhat recently emerging from their own history of being colonized by neighboring countries. That is a very long way of saying, Finns are Finns, for better or worse, until they are placed in contact with others – as the excerpt above says, 'national groups become understood as racial groups through immigration'.

Similarly to a few different countries covered thus far, Finland wasn't always the home of the 'smartest' kids or the 'happiest' citizens. As noted by Hoegaertes *et al.* (2022), it was a poor, farming country until the second half of the 20th century when it rose in prominence amid its industrialization. This coincides with their gradual acceptance in Western Europe and the United States, and of course, that acceptance can be equated to membership in the fraternity of whiteness. This rapid change contributes to a sense of cultural whiplash, wherein, as we've seen in places such as Algeria, because they considered themselves to have been victims of colonialism fairly recently, then they are not participating in further hierarchization within their borders. And the global apotheosis of the country as a homogeneous cultural utopia means there's little impetus to perform any sort of self-examination.

As Hoegaertes *et al.* (2022: 5) explained, 'Today, Finland can be defined as a "global winner": a modern Western welfare state ranking high on global indexes such as freedom of the press, gender equality, PISA and even happiness. In 2018, Finland was selected as the "goodest" [sic] country, topping the Good Country Index, which measures what each country in the world contributes to the good of humanity. … These notions feed into a sense of Finnish exceptionalism and a self-image as a country outside of colonial involvements or of the historical burden of racism'.

Well, that would be nice if it were true.

Reality

I spoke to Dr. Hanna Lind, a colleague who lives in Finland but is originally from Western Europe. She had some thoughts about racism in the 'goodest' country.

> So I think the last time we talked I would have maybe argued that the most dangerous form of racism that I see in Finland at the moment is

color-evasiveness, or silence around race, shying away from the topic, silencing minoritized racialized communities, indigenous communities or dismissing them. So kind of not dealing with it. But I think things have taken a turn to the worse, bad and terrible. And it's actually with the current political leadership. There's a lot of very explicit racism, very explicit exclusion and marginalization and aggression against minoritized and already vulnerable people. So I don't think I would say it like that anymore. I think what is really interesting in the Finnish case is that Finns as people born and raised here have actually themselves gone through some process of racialization as, I don't know, Irish people or Jewish people in the US like that. It's not so long ago that they weren't considered white themselves. So it's just another one of these nice cases, how quickly you can become white and yet how fragile that there is or unattainable that status is for others. ... It's one of my pet peeves that Finland is the more superior, more ethical, more multicultural, more bilingual, multilingual, more educated, better education system-having nation that's, I think it's a myth. I've also been trying to challenge that myth in several publications and I think my question would always be, why do you think that so if somebody says like, 'Finland has kind of a leg up on these things,' and I would always ask, like, 'why do you think that?' ... I think this reputation Finland has built as this educational model nation is making us complacent, and it's making us not see.

Dr. Lind covered a lot of what I previewed above, including the recent racialization process and how it mirrored that of other liminally white groups in the United States, as well as the darkness that I thought was still beneath the snowy surface but is apparently quite visible as their color-evasive shield has begun to thaw.

Now, she's asking a rhetorical question there, as to why Finns think they are superior on various metrics – it's because that's what the numbers say. As with almost every context mentioned in this book, the tyranny of quantitative research allows established status quos to go unchallenged, and there are those who won't even consider qualitative work and narratives as being of equal value. It's the stories that resonate, though, the stories that give color – *pun only sort of intended* – to a complex, human world. So if it's true – *and it is* – that their test scores are relatively strong, helping to create what is a somewhat new but nonetheless internationally popular master narrative about Finnish cultural superiority, then instead of other countries seeing their assessments and aiming to ape their attainment, we ought to listen to the stories to understand that much has been sacrificed to secure this crown.

To be clear, I am not going to pretend there is nothing good about Finland's culture when compared to others – paid family leave and gender equity are unequivocally good things to strive for. And even within the vaunted education system that I've come to view somewhat skeptically,

Dr. Lind did point out that some good has come of their international rankings, even if they can't actually prove why they've done so well. Accordingly, a correlation/causation confusion occurs internationally, and other nations assume that if they do some of what Finland does, they will achieve what Finland has. But education, and people in general, are messy and far from linear. I'll allow her to explain in more detail.

> I think the one thing that needs to be said more clearly about this is we don't actually know why the results were so good. They're also not that good anymore. But we don't actually know why. So nobody knows why they were good, right? We have no way to prove it. And so what happened though, is actually quite interesting and it's both good and bad. I think what happened after the good PISA results came for the first time is that people started to kind of freeze because there had been some some loud voices in Finland that were saying, like, 'we need private schools and we need more standardized testing and high stakes testing,' God knows what you know, and rankings and let's do all the things a lot of people are doing and I think that put a hold on that. So in some ways it saved us from a lot of these things that we know, corrupt school systems can create segregation and create exclusion and create disadvantages. In that way, it was not all bad, but I think it also created an atmosphere where we commodify education, sell our curricula, sell our school knowledge and not change anything because once it's working, everybody is afraid to touch it anymore, because it's like it's working. So let's not do anything. And in some sense, it was a good thing because we still don't have a terrible testing regime as in other places, and we still don't have school rankings as in other places. I wouldn't say it's not existent, but it's better than it could maybe be if it hadn't happened.

To follow up, because you read what she said and may misinterpret it – Finland does not ban all private education, it just cannot be run for profit and is publicly funded (European Commission, 2024). I'm not quite sure what makes them 'private' in that sense, but of course, people hear a version of this and say, aha, that's the problem, when it's always more complex than a silver bullet, even though I do think private schools, at least in their American conception, are largely problematic, having spent decades attending them before finally attending a public university for my doctorate and enjoying it more than any other experience I'd had.

It is in fact great that Finland doesn't have nearly as much high-stakes testing as the United States and other such places, though, as she said, this doesn't inherently explain their PISA (Programme for International Student Advancement) scores. Sure, they score relatively highly, but so does Japan, where testing is even higher-stress than in the United States. Ultimately, I believe people cherry-pick whatever matches their preferred narrative and run with that, all of which flattens a complex society into something as superficial as its best qualifies, thereby allowing for the complacency Dr. Lind described.

I asked her about Finland's supposed – *and government-codified* – homogeneity and she strongly disputed this reputation the country has gained for itself.

> The argument that actually comes up is, 'well, Finland is just not used to diversity,' it's like bullshit. Like Finland has always been diverse, has always been racially diverse, has always been linguistically diverse, has always been culturally diverse. There have always been Jewish people and Romani people and Sami people here. As long as this place has existed and been populated, it has been diverse in every way you can imagine. And just because people have for colonial and nationalistic reasons, decided not to see that diversity or violently suppress it, I think if you don't want to see diversity, you're not going to see it. And that doesn't matter if it hits you in the face. So that would be my take on that. … And so I think this, 'well you know, it's not racially diverse, so you're excused' is a very dangerous argument. I think the visibility of race argument is a dangerous one because not all racial difference is visible. Not to everybody in the same way.

Note that I cited statistics about language and nationality earlier in the chapter because that's the accepted data. Hearing these perspectives may just not matter to someone during cursory research about Finnish demographics – the government's decisions shape the narrative we all consume, and that certain powers are invested in upholding. I'm never going to convince anyone who agrees with the way Finns are currently categorized that they should be seen as more heterogeneous than they are perceived as, and I'd argue that part of that is the value of being included in the frigid embrace of whiteness (and yes that's my final ice/snow joke, but they've won enough Winter Olympics medals, they'll be okay).

Accordingly, as I've said many times, whiteness is about much more than skin color, and there are many shades within it. Almost everyone with a Finnish passport might be racialized as white in the United States or the United Kingdom, but inside of Finland, there is no hesitation to uphold hierarchies that may not be visible from our distant vantage point. The top of the educational and cultural mountain may seem far from where we stand, but I've no reason to think they are free from participating in the same avalanche of oppression under which so many of us are hopelessly buried.

(Okay, *that's* the last snow joke.)

What Needs to Happen

I know that this book is, essentially, a comparison of countries, but, we need to stop comparing countries in metrics such as education.

As Finland shows, even when countries perform well, there are far too many complex factors involved for the comparison to hold much predictive weight. In populations of the tens of millions, or more, there's never going to be a singular answer for why anything happens, so the only result is a reliance upon stereotypes, heuristics and assumptions. Accordingly, people know what little they know about a place like Finland – *hence my snow jokes* – and then they compare that to what they feel about their own country, and the hierarchies are laid bare. Finland has X, but we have Y, so we would be more like them if we did that one thing. For some people, it's positive actions like working against high-stakes testing, but then, given that other highly scoring countries have that practice, it's hard to justify, and so in the United States we have done little to alter our behavior. Without more effective analysis, the supposed homogeneity is elevated, and as such the global racial hierarchy is reified silently for those who have yet to break free from the narrative we've all been fed.

Let's hear what Dr. Lind has to say:

> I think what I hear in research contexts where I talked to a more diverse audience of parents would be a surface level agreement or appreciation of multicultural education. Or multilingual education, because that's kind of my area. And if you scratch the surface, this rather naive, celebratory kind of approach to education, 'okay, let's have multicultural people there.' But yet if you scratch it a bit, then it's very clear that what kind of what kind of multiculturalism that is, so that it does not mean like migrants from the global south or refugees from socioeconomically disadvantaged or exploited countries or it does not mean like, it does not mean people who need support or who think about things differently or who question us in our ways, but you know, we like them migrants as long as they bring us nice food and funny things to wear and that kind of stuff. So I don't know … I think that discourses of whiteness are so absurd in a way because it is so easy to fall from grace with whiteness as grace. You know what I mean? Like I mean, it's so easy in Finland to choose to step in the wrong direction and become questioned or undermined as a member of the white community. You know, like for example, like, Russia decides it wants to make an imperial move and attacks Ukraine. You are a Russian speaking person, but not from Russia. But let's say you're from, I don't know, Estonia, have nothing to do with Russia, if anything an anti-Russian attitude because you're from Estonia. And you get attacked because you speak Russian and suddenly everything falls apart, your good immigrant status, your model minority status. That is questionable in the first place, but suddenly you're not considered a legitimate member here of the community or a white person or a valuable member of the society because your race or your language has identified you as lesser on the racial hierarchy. Racioinguistic

ideologies snap into place right away. And so your whiteness becomes fragile. None of this you have caused in any way, just because the sociopolitical situation has shifted in that way. So, if you open your eyes, this is not just the story of one individual but this is Finnish history, full of the stories of things like that happening to communities, to cities, to areas to peoples and so like, I don't know how you cannot see that, how ridiculous this concept of whiteness is, because in this short amount of time that the Finnish nation-state has existed. It has fallen apart for so many and then been rebuilt and falling apart again. It makes sense as long as it benefits somebody right? But like, if you open your eyes a little bit, then it must be clear that that whiteness has no, no logic outside of power and domination.

I'll leave it there.

12 Lacking the Tools

Italy

Background

Getting close to the end here. This is the final chapter for which I conducted an interview, the reason for which will become obvious when you consider the context of the chapter that follows, and although scheduling (mostly) academics, with absurd schedules, in many different time zones, while also scheduling interviews for the previous book I completed, is not for the faint of heart, getting to this point in the book is an interesting place to pause and reflect.

As I've said a million times by now, I don't know that I wanted to have to write this book – and I know I didn't *have to* in the sense that I was the one who proposed it, but you get what I mean. My first book felt incomplete and narrow as more time passed, and, to use another pop culture reference, if you've ever seen the end of the movie *8 Mile*, I try to use my writing the way the main character does, anticipating criticisms and including them in the text so that they are necessarily weakened and hopefully stunned into silence like that film's antagonist. As with rap battles, I consider my writing to be more of a dialogue and an interlocking series of narratives, but when I put my first book into the world, I hadn't any idea what the response would be, and I anticipated criticisms mostly related to my slightly sweaty and overthought framing device regarding the symptoms of Antisocial Personality Disorder. But people seemed to like that structure, and mostly I received comments that it was a bit too American, and too Justin-centric. Now, I simply don't have the capability to write a story I'm not a main character in, but by now you'd've stopped reading if that bothered you. As for the 'too American' part, I do hope that the comparisons and contrasts I've drawn thus far help shade in – *ha!* – the picture more effectively than in my previous work.

I say all this here to say that, there's one angle I believe I haven't quite covered here, which is a group of people whose position within the broader master narrative is so widely known, at least in a superficial way. Despite what xenophobic horrors I'm sure have continued to occur in the time since I wrote these words – *or even while I wrote this sentence* – we still, as a nation, like to pound our chests and crow about how we're a 'melting pot', comprised of various groups of (the right kind of) immigrants. We talk about Ellis Island, and wax poetic about the way various communities pulled themselves up by their bootstraps – *a phrase that is actually meant to be a joke, given you cannot pull yourself up by your bootstraps if you are wearing said boots; think about it* – but we gloss over who was allowed to thrive, and who we've still kept on the lower rungs of our hierarchies. And, with the exception of maybe the Irish, there's perhaps no community that best exemplifies the path from exclusion to tentative inclusion maintained by allegiance to power structures in the United States than those who emigrated here from Italy. Perhaps our most revered and respected film export – *The Godfather* – was a pulpy airport novel elevated into grandeur, helping to crystallize this portion of the master narrative for all to consume, not that I'm accusing Francis Ford Coppola of ulterior motives.

However, this chapter isn't really about Italian-American immigrants, per se. But I did want to think of that part of the story when considering raciolinguistic ideologies in Italy, as well as how they have and haven't been transported across the pond by the people who came to our shores and their progeny.

Perception

As was the case with California, I've written about all this before, the only difference being that I actually conducted an interview this time. But before I get to that, let's just hear what past me (Gerald, 2022) had to say regarding the process via which Irish and Italian immigrants to the United States managed to access whiteness, starting in the 19th century:

The Irish were being used as 'Swiss guards of slave power' (Ignatiev, 1995: 162), which angered the country's nativist faction. Irish voting blocs helped elect Philadelphia's new mayor, who in turn rewarded them with powerful positions in city government, including police commissioner. As Ignatiev (1995: 163) explained, 'The Irish cop is more than a quaint symbol. His appearance on the city police marked a turning point in Philadelphia in the struggle of the Irish to gain the rights of white men. It meant thereafter that the Irish would be officially empowered (armed) to defend themselves from the nativist mobs, and at the same time to carry out their own agenda against Black people.' Italians followed a path similar to the Irish, enduring racial slurs, 'consigned the church pews set aside for black people' (Staples, 2019), before gaining power through policing. After all, police needed to do their duty, to protect and serve order, and that order meant whiteness.

Now. Look. That was an angrier book than this one. I have since aged a few years. And it's from a section about how policing and the subjugation of Black bodies is a tantalizing ticket to whiteness for groups previously excluded. I don't particularly want to relitigate that, as I've already made that point four years ago, and also because I don't feel all that righteous wagging my finger at the moral compromises made by groups that had been pushed to the margins. I am not, by any means, excusing this process, as if these communities had no agency in their ascendance, but to me there's a sadness to all of this, that I would like to unpack, particularly with respect to Italians, but also the Irish, given I'm married into a partially Italian family and am also, apparently, 1/16th Irish.

First, the pop culture angle. I mentioned *The Godfather* earlier, and there's a scene in the movie where the otherwise sophisticated gangsters at the center of the film look down on the trafficking of narcotics, not necessarily because it's immoral – *these are murderers, after all* – but because it's beneath them, and best associated with what the character calls 'the dark people'. Now, the primary protagonists don't quite use this language, and indeed the character in question is meant to be seen as unpleasant, but, first of all, audiences are not particularly skilled at nuance, and secondly, this ties back into the overall theme of this book, that overt, direct racism is the province of the Bad People, not the polite corners of society, even if said society is organized crime.

You see this in other depictions of these two immigrant groups. In the TV show *The Knick*, about an early 20th century New York City hospital, one episode focuses on a racist riot, wherein the Irish of lower Manhattan become enraged, over some trumped up misunderstanding, and chase after the Black residents of the area. In *Gangs of New York – made by another Italian-American from Little Italy* – the 1863 'draft riots' are depicted, in which Irish immigrants engaged in four days of violent, racist behavior toward Black city residents. Even if some of the stories are fiction or fictionalized, enough of this is based on real history that it's not necessarily being embellished, but I do want to circle back to what is being depicted, and how it relates to the overall story we've all been fed.

I am by no means saying these things shouldn't have been dramatized – I think they are vital to understand. But just like the American South is the Mount Olympus of American racism, when we manage to be slightly more honest about these hierarchies in the major and more diverse metropolises of the Northeast, it's still never the, let's say, friendly K-12 teacher overly scrutinizing a rambunctious Black boy, or something else mundane but deeply impactful and harmful. Yes, it's harder to make these silent decisions compelling on screen – *it works better in text* – and artists such as Coppola and Scorsese are often trying to examine their own heritage with a critical eye. The problem isn't what they've chosen to do, but that, first of all, as members of these communities, they're the ones who have the responsibility of addressing this issue, and second, that members of groups that didn't relatively recently attain the status of 'white' don't feel the urgency to be more reflective. As such, unless you put considerable effort into analyzing these topics, the narrative you receive is that the racism worth fearing in the Northeast is from communities that arrived here more recently, and while that's not *un*true in the case of the police, it places groups that ought to be working in solidarity in direct, violent opposition to one another, which I suppose is the whole point of the master narrative in the first place.

And then there's the perception I myself have in the areas where I've spent the most time. Be it New York, New Jersey, Philadelphia, Boston, these are places I know quite well, for one reason or another. And if I can be honest with you, the places I personally fear for both myself and my young sons are the parts of these cities that are populated with some of these communities. I actually live in a somewhat Italian-American area now, but as a homeowner, I feel comfortable enough. On the other hand, between my first and final drafts of this book, I did get pulled over by the police for no particular reason a few blocks from my house, so, joke's on me I guess.

But when I hear stories about police killings in and around New York, or random acts of violence from one citizen to another, and I take note of who's involved, I genuinely worry. It's not the South I fear. It's the neighborhoods that fear people who look like me, which have always been nearby. You can Google these places yourself, but I do my best to avoid Bensonhurst, Howard Beach and particularly Staten Island, because they do not want me there, and I am happy to oblige their request.

I'll get more into that in the final chapter, of course, but, suffice it to say, part of my hope with this portion is to disabuse myself of these preconceived notions. So my interlocutor has some work to do.

Reality

I spoke to Dr. Caterina Romandini, a professor at an NYC University who works in language studies, and a native of Italy. Here's the first bit of what she told me:

> The idea is that the first form of racialization or idea of different race was within the context of Italy was with the Southerners. So the idea that people in the South were a little bit African and that made them lazy, you know, inferior or more inclined to be upset and you know, many, many stereotypes that you often see associated with people. What I understand is that during the first wave of colonialism, in the late 1800s, it was under the king but then there was a second wave under fascism. And at that point, the racial discourse was, first of all, fascism didn't immediately talk about race. It was more about this attempt to create national unity by also elevating a more rural ways of living in the South, as truly Italian and you know, it is remembered like having a lot of kids in countries. In some ways that elevated Italian Southerners to being not as Black as the people in the colonies that we are going to colonize. So we see that hierarchies of you know, both color and race in ways that are defined obviously, via discourse, you know, it's not a real thing.

Of course it's not. It's worth noting that, although I'm sort of hopskotching around the globe and through various periods of somewhat recent history, there is obviously a massive temporal overlapping going on here. None of these countries were operating in a vacuum, so although this chapter is separated from that of the one on Algeria by several pages, one has to remember that much of what Dr. Romandini described was even closer to them, geographically, than their exploitative relationship with France. And, in my lengthy sojourn into pop culture in the previous section, it is also worth noting that the people who embodied said upwardly mobile master narrative were often Southern Italians who had fled their home country because of some of what she explained here. In a way, a part of this racial narrative impacted a wave of immigration that, in turn, infiltrated the rungs of power in the United States and helped maintain the racial order here. Sometimes history just feels like a waterfall we're all rolling over in a little barrel.

Anyway.

The generation of my grandma *[note: referring to the World War Two period]* went from not having to eat literally nothing but polenta, which is cornmeal, basically, to having a refrigerator and running motor. So those were like, in five years, your life it's upside down. So this to say that the idea of our people racializing was never part of the big reflection, and in recent years it came out, and it came out because we have a growing number of Black Italians. So I see very different responses to skin color, depending on, you know, how you're perceived. So for example, if you're American and 'cool' and you look like the videos that you fantasize about sometimes, this Black consumption. So if you're perceived like that, then you're considered a different type compared to the people who migrate to the Mediterranean risking their lives or, you know, come in really, really different ways but at the same time, that the line between the two is very narrow.

I'll get back to the 'cool Americans' part shortly, but I wanted to zero in on her comment about the growing number of Black Italians. It's true, though the numbers are fuzzy for reasons that will shortly become clear. From a news article about this community's experience and struggles:

Today, notions of national belonging in Italy center on whiteness, even in the country's citizenship law. The country does not grant nationality based on being born within Italian borders, but rather on bloodline. In practice, this means that the great grandchild of an Italian who migrated to Argentina, even if she or he does not speak Italian and has never set foot in Italy, faces fewer bureaucratic hurdles to get Italian citizenship than the child of African nationals who was born and schooled in Italy, and who speaks only Italian with a local accent to boot. Those in the latter's situation only have a year to apply for citizenship once they turn 18, but the process is riddled with pedantic bureaucracy that many consider institutional racism. (Soguel, 2022)

Fun. Accordingly, considering that the country barely considers them Italian, it's hard to pin down what their actual population is, but they are there, and they are real, and fighting to be seen as legitimate.

Dr. Romandini explained accordingly:

People who were raised in Italy, many of them born in Italy, went to Italian schools, and still struggle, especially if their parents were not citizens. They are denied citizenship when they turn 18. So you basically have some sort of protection until you're a minor but the moment you turn 18 you're effectively telling them, the only thing you've known in your own life, you know everything about Italy because you were there the whole time. And then you suddenly need a work permit and visa to stay in Italy.

Back to the 'cool American' thing. It's interesting how these stereotypes are spread globally. Obviously class status is a factor here, as the migrants from North Africa are braving the sea for a chance at freedom rather than visiting a fashion show in Milan. Americans, partially because of the very popular culture I've continuously highlighted, are assumed to be generally wealthy, and it's certainly true that the ones who visit Europe need to possess a certain amount of disposable income to do so. Every time I've been to Europe, they assume I'm African until I speak, and then they instantly reclassify me, which is useful in the moment because they're usually nicer, but discomforting upon reflection. It's part of the reason I've avoided the continent for a long time.

This is not limited to Italy, or to Europe. If you've never met someone who looks a certain way – *race is not just color, but color is a heuristic we use for it* – your response is influenced by the images you've received. So these same assumptions occur all around the world where Black faces are relatively rare, the difference being the proximity to an underclass from which everyone hopes to remain separate. And ultimately, when I say 'open my mouth' with regard to how I, or we, are seen, I mean English. English is a shortcut to class-based assumptions, especially for those in otherwise minoritized groups, even if not inherently a shortcut to actual membership in higher classes. These raciolinguistic ideologies shape how we're perceived regardless of where we go, or where we try to prove that we belong.

And finally, she reflected on how these assumptions impacted her own experience when she originally moved to the United States. Indeed, what she shared here is the flipside of our blaming all of racism on the American South, because we're also, implicitly, saying that the story of racism is history we've learned from. The racism in which we exist currently involves all the different types mentioned throughout this book, yet because of how we've attempted to portray ourselves, people move here with quite the wrong impression.

> So when I came here I had from what I saw on TV and representation and this was, you know, 20 years ago, so we didn't get George Floyd or Black Lives Matter. On TV. I might, you know, you've now might have a different perspective about the US but I I thought it was a post-racial society. I thought, you know, I knew the history and I was glad that history was over because now you know, there's no segregation. So I was really shocked that the circles I gravitated to were all white and I said, what's going on here? I look back to then, and I remember, you know, noticing this was this huge segregation. And then as a teacher, especially noticing the different access to resources in my institution, which is predominantly white. It's less predominantly white now, but still predominantly white. When I arrived, it was overwhelmingly white and whenever I had one single Black student in class, then it just didn't look normal to me. I grew up in an environment where no jokes about Black people were made, you know, there was no hate in my household and everybody was, it was a lot of rhetoric on, 'we all are people,' that we should be judged individually as people are not judged, I would say, but you know, so I definitely didn't have that type of preconceived notion. But I noticed that I didn't have the tools to understand and interact with people who went through a very different walk of life.

As an educator, I find this to be one of the tragic parts of the entire story I'm trying to tell in this book. Moreso even than the countries fooling themselves about their own lack of complicity, for someone with, now, a doctorate and an educator career, to be admittedly woefully educated about reality is a stark reminder that if we are to make any progress on these issues in the future, our educators, be they in Italy or the United States, will need to be taught by people who, themselves, were taught effectively. And I'm pretty sure there's a strong faction of people working very hard to prevent that from occurring, and one of them is in the White House as I write this, but we don't need to dwell on that.

What Needs to Happen

Dr. Romandini pointed out that relying upon American thought can harm possible progress in discourse on said topics in Italy. She notes that at the very least they do consume and engage with the work of authors of color now, but it's rarely contemporary, and often ignores what modern Italian scholars are attempting to put forth on the issue. 'What I see now', she said, 'is the discourse on race in Italy is dominated by what comes from the States because of how, you know, social media is easy to access, but also translation of authors. So the same authors who were read here 10 years ago, 15 years ago, have been bred now in Italy as a model, which is incomplete because we have these Italian scholars who study race, who can really add to the understanding of what's going on.'

Accordingly, I would say that, no matter how 'behind' many of the locations I've written about are, the fact that there are people willing to share their perspective with me means that there's always someone trying to push the conversation forward, push past the master narrative both within the country and with regard to the global raciolinguistic discussion. Not only does everyone need to try and re-learn something other than the public pedagogy put forth to all of us, but we need to seek out and proliferate the ideas generated by those within each context who are at the vanguard of the discourse. And, I would add, not just for Italy, but everywhere, we need to do whatever we can to get these ideas outside of the little bubble of academia. I'll come back to this in the conclusion, but if a progressive racial or linguistic idea falls in the forest – *that is, is published in an exclusive journal* – and no one is around to hear it – *that is, it's impossible to access* – then does it make a sound? If it does, if it manages to gain even the smallest public foothold, it's still drowned out by all the noise we've been subjected to throughout our lives.

13 Home Sweet Home?

New York City

Background

As I said in the last chapter and in previous ones, I was told directly that this book couldn't just be about me, and that makes sense. I have a whole other line of scholarship that is mostly personal education and neurodivergence stories, and I needed to cast a wider net this time. But all of these ideas descend from my own experiences, and therefore, now that you've heard from everyone I've interviewed, I thought it important to ground you in how all of this came about. And I don't really mean career-wise in this case – I mean the master narrative that I myself was sold – *and that I unfortunately bought into* – as I came of age.

As a child, I had just about the same perception as everyone else. In fifth grade specifically, we read some young adult novel about racism in the South, and the teacher asked us what our impressions of the region were. People said a lot of things, but the most common refrain was 'stupid'. I don't necessarily blame these 9-to-11-year-olds for having this mindset, to be clear, but I wanted to bring it up to clarify that these narratives start early and are solidified before the age when critical analysis is to be expected. Instead of just learning about both a region and a concept, we actually have to unlearn what we've been fed and replace it with new knowledge, twice the task of considering a new line of thought.

My father, who was born and raised in those contexts of which I speak, was very clear and honest with me about his reality. He didn't mean to imply I should look out for such things exclusively, but I was a kid, and because, especially being neurodivergent, I didn't understand social situations very well, the longer I went without subtle, institutional racism making itself apparent to me, the more I believed that Jim Crow white hood racism of the Southern variety was all that existed.

This isn't to say I never was called a 'nigger'. One time, I had set up a date with someone near the house my mom moved to when I was in college, and this was an ex-urban part of Pennsylvania, so when she and her friends got on the phone to call me that word, I was briefly shaken, but told myself, well, I guess that can happen in these areas.

Another time, I was right across the street from my dad's apartment in Manhattan, visiting a record store, which is a thing humans used to do, for all you young readers out there. I had nothing I really wanted to buy, it was just something I did to pass the time when I didn't have social plans, and since I rarely had social plans as a teenager, I was there a lot. Anyway, via a misunderstanding, I didn't realize an elderly woman thought I was ignoring her when in fact I hadn't known she was talking to me, and her response, muttered under her breath but not quietly, was, 'can't even hear, the little nigger'. Other people around looked at me, the signal for 'so what do you want to do about this', but it didn't seem of much use. Frankly, I was just happy others supported me, even if silently. But, again, this was a senior citizen, whose mind may not have been 'all there', and it didn't seem to be a New York City problem.

Finally, at one of my jobs, when I worked at a senior center, one of my tasks was to announce the numbers for lunch – *look, these are the things that happen at senior centers* – and because I like speaking publicly, I would never just stick to the script. In one of my ad-libs, I referred to the entire audience as 'guys', which is, indeed, technically sexist even if the term is often not gendered, and one woman came up to me angrily to tell me I shouldn't have said that. I acknowledged my mistake and tried to move on, but her response was to escalate, and ask, 'how would you feel if I called you a nigger?'

Again, I was supported by my surroundings. Other seniors looked at me, and an elderly Black woman talked to me about it, clearly with her having been through much worse. I went into my office and told my colleagues, who quickly wrote up a report and got the woman banned from the place, and I never saw her again. Even the entire executive team came to find me to tell me they supported me, not that I had been worried, but it was nice.

All of this is to say, it's not that I thought racism didn't exist in New York City, between my experiences and what I read about the police, but it always seemed like an outlier or an anomaly, and not something that was ingrained into the way the place was organized.

I, uh, wasn't right about all of that.

Perception

For most of my childhood and adolescence, my father lived on the West Side of Manhattan and my mother lived in Brooklyn. Though it's unbelievably expensive now, when he actually moved into his apartment in the early 1970s, his neighborhood wasn't all that fancy. It was closer to the bombed-out landscape depicted in both versions of *West Side Story* – *that's why the movie is called that, after all* – and the wonderfully ornate concert hall at Lincoln Center hadn't yet been renovated and returned to glory, like a lot of what was true of New York in that decade. But that was before my time there.

By the time my memory starts, the West Side was where *Seinfeld* took place, a region that was, as far as I could tell from my child eyes, fairly well mixed and friendly. The people in my building were a motley crew of all colors, nationalities and religions, and I never felt out of place. It was definitely trending toward more wealth and exclusivity, but, and I have brought this up in other chapters, the centrality of public transportation really shaped my perception. There was simply no way to avoid seeing people who looked different from you, spoke differently from you, if you were all crammed into the one train and complaining about delays together. We would even occasionally see celebrities walking around, because the ones who live in New York mostly seemed to try and live their lives fairly normally, particularly if they were not A-list superstars. Frequently, we'd pass Broadway actors or those who'd had bit parts on TV shows that filmed in the city. We didn't have a lot of space, my Dad and I, but I felt comfortable.

My mother and I first lived in an area called Cobble Hill when I was born, but we moved out of there when I was three so I can't really comment, except to note that, like every place I'll mention in this chapter, it's unaffordable in the present day. We then moved, briefly, to Brooklyn Heights, the neighborhood where my private school was located, which is more exclusive than every other place I've lived, but then we settled in what realtors now call lots of different things, but is best described as the border between Flatbush and Midwood, fairly deep into Brooklyn. In fact, it was far enough away from my school that certain parents wouldn't let their kids have playdates at my home, a signal toward one of the points I'll be making in the 'reality' section that follows. Eventually, the lack of visits made me lonely in my teenage years, but we're not there yet.

Anyway, we lived in an old (1904), large house, and it felt to me as though we had the perfect spot. In terms of culture, if you walked in one direction, you'd find yourself in an area that was populated by immigrant communities from the Caribbean – *the vast majority of whom were Black* – and if you walked in another direction, it was a heavily Jewish area. Precisely where we lived, there were a lot of Italian-Americans mixed in with the other groups. I heard lots of languages, saw people of every stripe and it felt like the ideal that New York had always presented itself as, a place welcome to all groups that features an area for everyone who wants it. Obviously, with the prices having since skyrocketed – *I sure couldn't afford to buy my own former house if I'd wanted to* – the population has changed to a certain extent, but when I briefly visited a few years ago, the flavor wasn't as dramatically different as I feared, which was heartening.

I remember that I was confused when I found out about the concept of a 'minority' and that I supposedly was one. I knew there weren't many kids who looked like me at my school, but I didn't live near there, and, as far as I could tell from both my relatives and my environs, I didn't stand out. Frankly, if we stood out in any way, it was that we had relatively higher incomes than the nearby Black communities, which sometimes got me teased for being a nerd, which, to be clear, I was. But that had very little to do with the ideologies this book is about. Suffice it to say, I was learning the same master narratives that we all were, from both the public pedagogy of popular culture and my school, a supposedly progressive institution that eschewed competition and letter grades and therefore felt it was morally superior. The Bad Racist Place was the South, the Bad Racist Time was in the past, and I had no reason to suspect anything else.

I first gained some vague awareness of police brutality in 1997, when a Haitian immigrant named Abner Louima was brutalized – *though he survived* – in my very neighborhood (Chan, 2007). You can read up on the details if you're unfamiliar, but it was clear cut, it was egregious, and he won a massive settlement from the city after suing them. The officer who was the primary aggressor – *whose name was actually Justin, in an unfortunate coincidence for me* – was sentenced to 30 years in prison, an extremely rare case for such a conviction and punishment (he was released in 2023). The lesson I could have received from this having occurred essentially in my backyard was the one I later figured out about how vigilant I needed to be about not enraging said officers, especially in New York, but the only thing I understood at the time was that this other Justin Was Bad, that sometimes Bad Things Happen and that justice had been served given Louima's recovery, settlement and successful ongoing status as an activist and philanthropist. I was probably too young to understand the nuances of all of this, but that's sort of my point: we're all fed the same story about where racism – *and, in Louima's case, xenophobia and linguistic ideologies* – lives, and that story is that it lives elsewhere in others who mean to cause harm. This renders us both ignorant and also somewhat powerless to seek true equity. Indeed, even now, as I'll say more about in the conclusion, I by no means believe that having been taught these narratives makes any of us bad or inherently hateful – I just believe we can all tell a more accurate story. That, however, requires us to see our environment for what it actually is, and it took me until my adulthood to see New York City with clarity and honesty.

Reality

By the time I was in my 30s, I was living in Queens with my wife. Queens County is one of the most diverse regions of any city in the world, with innumerable languages spoken, and people of all creeds and backgrounds. Though a white former colleague of mine sneered when I told her I was moving there – *again, signals I should have paid attention to* – I was proud to be a resident of the borough, and settled into a routine that worked for me. Once our first son was imminent, I was hoping against hope that we'd find a way to raise him there, around so many different cultures, cuisines and customs. And then the pandemic happened.

Now, in case you don't remember, New York was one of the places hit hardest by the early waves of COVID-19. Just a few weeks into our son's life, we were in a high-rise looking down at a constant stream of ambulances all day and night, unable to bring him to meet any relatives who hadn't been lucky enough to see him in his first few days out of the hospital. It seems like ancient history now, but there was a sense of camaraderie during a uniquely scary time, with all of the communitarian slogans – *'stay home, save lives'* – and shuttered schools and businesses. Obviously, this cooperation wasn't going to last forever, but I was probably a bit too hopeful we'd come out of our shared experience chastened and improved as a city, and as a world. My own side career as someone who writes and speaks about these issues started during lockdown, as I've mentioned, and none of my books would exist without my having been trapped inside like everyone else, gaining a small audience on social media and in my corner of the academic world. I even began teaching online courses of my own design about the ways race and whiteness impacted society, and conducted interviews with participants as the primary data source for my dissertation later on.

So, where I was living in Queens at the time was a neighborhood called Long Island City (LIC). Queens is technically a part of Long Island – *along with Brooklyn, and Nassau and Suffolk counties* – but it's also part of New York City, making it somewhat confusing that Long Island City is neither an actual city nor is it considered 'Long Island'. In fact, LIC is the part of Queens closest to Manhattan and therefore farthest away from Long Island. No, it doesn't make any sense.

Anyway, LIC used to be mostly unpopulated and full of warehouses. Over time, developers realized that its proximity to Manhattan meant it was a prime location for apartments, especially given how many subway trains ran through the area. My commute to my midtown office was actually only 15 minutes, for example.

During COVID, this meant I spent a lot of days walking in slow circles around the streets that were still mostly warehouses, trying to stay 'socially distant', pushing a stroller or holding my dog's leash. It was isolating, like a lot of the pandemic, but as restrictions began to lift, I was excited for things to return to 'normal'. I think, as we all now know, they never did and never will.

The thing about everyone staying home is that the people who didn't have permanent homes were suddenly much more visible. And so when people did venture out, visible poverty was unavoidable, especially in a city where people don't tend to drive cars as often. The rhetoric from right-wing sources grew more and more hysterical, and the crime rate did increase – *though it subsequently decreased, to no one's surprise* – leading to heightened fears of violence and danger. New York also received an influx of migrants from Central and South America – *many of whom were bussed in from right-wing states to prove a point* – and so we were suddenly in a situation where struggling individuals and families were common sights, almost all of whom were people of color, and most of whom spoke other languages.

And I thought we'd handle it better.

People moved out in 2020 as home prices plummeted, and those who stayed were bombarded with discourse about migrants and others without permanent homes. Surely, I figured, we'd be immune to this sort of baiting. This was New York. Even though it was inarguably true that our resources were strained after COVID, and that a lot of people were watching their incomes dwindle, we'd be better than the people who allowed themselves to be tricked into blaming 'external threats' for their situations. But New Yorkers are people just like everyone else, and part of why I wrote this book was to point out that every place, even if it's one that claims to be welcoming, is susceptible to the influence of raciolinguistic ideologies, whether they want to be or not. People I otherwise respected would whisper about the migrants, about how many of them were being added to public schools and how this would make things hard for their own children, about how the subway was unsafe to ride now, about how they couldn't wait to leave.

Meanwhile, with the work both my wife and I did at the time in housing-related nonprofits, we could hear how hard it was for people to afford places to live, so even the people who weren't muttering under their breath about migrants were saying legitimate things about the skyrocketing costs of the city. Eventually, it got to us, too, and when we decided we were going to have another child, we realized that, unless we wanted to stuff more and more people into a tiny apartment, we were going to need more space, and that space was going to have to come elsewhere.

I'd always wanted any children I had to be New Yorkers. As my family was descended from enslaved people, and both of my parents had been raised in other cities, I was the first in my family to be born in the city, and I wanted to establish a legacy. I have never felt the United States was truly my home, but New York always was, and I wanted to share this with whomever I ended up raising. Until all of these things happened in the early 2020s, I always told myself we were better than other places because everyone was welcome here. I'm not sure how I could see all these other places with as clear a vision as I hope I've conveyed throughout this book, yet be unable to be honest about New York, but, as many of these interviews have shown, it's hard for people to admit that the place that created them was stuck inside the same master narrative as everywhere else.

It broke my heart to leave – *and we didn't exactly go very far, we live five miles north of the city limits, and I still work in Manhattan* – but we did. We found a house and we left. The financial argument made sense, sure, but if I was honest with myself, and I'm trying to be, the New York City I loved only really existed inside of my head in the first place.

This was a city where every ethnicity had an enclave it could be proud of, from Jackson Heights to Woodlawn to my old neighborhood of Flatbush, and yes, even those areas I admitted I myself was scared of in Staten Island. This was a city with the neighborhood of Jamaica, Queens, which has little to do with the country of the same name but is full of immigrants from the Caribbean all the same, as well as sizeable groups of Asians and Latinos. Indeed, Jamaica is barely 3% white (Census, 2024).

But now, looking at the city from nearby, I realize that New York isn't just the city that has areas like Jamaica. It's also the city that has areas like its next door neighbor, Jamaica Estates. You know who's from Jamaica? Popular musicians such as 50 Cent, Nicki Minaj and members of Run-DMC. You know who's from Jamaica Estates? Donald Trump.

What Needs to Happen

As I write this, some absolute nonsense is happening targeting those very migrants and other struggling people we've chosen to use as scapegoats for issues actually caused by the behavior of oligarchs, so by the time this book is actually released, the city could look quite different. We're always going to have those areas where different cultures thrive, but maybe we can't actually live a fully harmonious and integrated life, because we just end up turning on each other when things become challenging. I think there's plenty of money to support everyone in the city if we actually felt like providing a living wage, and there are always efforts underway despite the heavy headwinds. But from where I sit, just north of town in Yonkers – *a smaller city with its own ugly history of racism* – NYC is probably always going to be kind of a mess. And maybe that's okay. Because I wonder if being honest with ourselves is the only way we're going to make any progress whatsoever toward fighting against the fictional stories we tell ourselves that keep us trapped in the hierarchies we cling to.

I don't really know, honestly. But I wouldn't be writing this book if it weren't for everything New York City has given me, all the bad and good all the same, so I just hope we can someday get closer to what we think we are.

Conclusion

So we come to the end, which is usually how these things work. A lot of stories were shared in the previous 13 chapters, and an overall shape was, I hope, put forth. I would like to end this by providing my own overall analysis and what I feel are the best things we can do to address all of this, something that I wouldn't quite say is innate to humanity but is unfortunately so ingrained that it might as well be. In other words, we're never really eradicating raciolinguistic ideologies, and there will always be some form of hierarchization in human society, but we can move away, to some extent, from the stories we've all been told. Before I offer my suggestions, though, let's review.

Recap

The **Pacific Northwest** is not the progressive paradise it presents itself as, and this shield of an image forestalls actual honesty and action. Oregon, in particular, started as a state that explicitly excluded Black residents, and far too little has been done to educate its current citizens on this past, let alone grappling with the results of these policies. Like New England, its relative lack of minoritized racial groups is a telling sign of how welcome folks like me tend to feel among its environs. We need far fewer 'Walls of Moms' and much more time spent listening to and centering other voices.

I've actually noticed from discourse among Canadian acquaintances that post-2025 oppressive events in the United States have provided **Canada** with yet another excuse to paint themselves as more moral than we are, which is exactly what they don't need to be doing. As this book hopefully makes clear, there is no purely good or bad place, and certainly no member of the Commonwealth that has engaged in settler colonialism has much of a leg to stand on at all. I reiterate that the residential schools closed when I was in, as Canadians would say, Grade 5, and despite the gray on my chin, I'm just not that old.

Along similar lines, but to perhaps a greater extent given its status as a progenitor, the **United Kingdom** needs to fully own up to its past, including its role in the slave trade that it's far too proud of exiting all of one year more quickly than the United States. Its primary territory having shrunk to a few small islands allows them to quietly continue to profit – *literally and ideologically* – off of what it has wrought, and to turn its head away from its impact that is still being felt in countries from A to Z. It certainly won't help if they continue to release self-analysis that paints them in a positive light wherein all their sins have been relegated to the past.

Australia's relative isolation means that for many of us reading this, we just don't know or see what they're up to. The fact that a policy as explicit as 'White Australia' existed for so long – *and wasn't actually hidden but was in fact centrally positioned* – yet even for someone like me who has spent however much time pondering these issues, I was completely unaware probably says something about me, but also about what they've gotten away with. Indeed, the closer you look at their relationship to both race and language, the more you can see that they're following exactly the same patterns as the country from the previous chapter that originally sent their outcasts there.

Unlike many of the previous places listed, **California** is actually relatively diverse, more so than almost any other context covered in the entire book. So that's good. And they tend to be leaders in progressive lip service. But ultimately, their biggest impact on the rest of us with regard to these issues is the soft power they wield through their industries, including both the technology produced via Silicon Valley and also their position as the primary purveyor of our public pedagogy. Until we all had social media – *which, again, is also largely California-derived* – many of us learned about other cultures through the shorthand of popular culture, myself included, and so their biggest need is addressing what they're teaching everyone about the world, whether or not they're intending to do so.

The very impetus for the vital research on 'sundown towns' and their prevalence outside of the American South, **the Midwest** changes the world every four years via our presidential elections, and presents itself as nice to ward off any cultural criticism. This is somewhat true of every place covered in this book, but I would argue that the contrast between the gentle stereotypes and brutal reality is one of the starkest. It's going to require not being very nice to address this dichotomy, and, perhaps ironically, in this case, it would in fact be very kind not to be nice.

In the United States, we've done a great deal of shaping the global image of **Mexico**, both through our cultural exports and media, positioning them as beneath us in every way. Accordingly, the hierarchies within the country aren't all that well known outside of those who live there or have a specific familiarity with said issues. Here, we paint them all as dangerous criminals, mostly with darker skin, but, aside from that being both racist and incorrect, the idea that a country of more than 100 million is a monolith just helps keep the people in power within Mexico separate from the populations who might otherwise receive more support.

The apotheosis of what the English as a Foreign Language industry has become since the late 20th century, **South Korea** and **Japan** are very different cultures that nonetheless engage with English and whiteness in similar ways, and it doesn't help that Westerners engage with both countries similarly too, hence the combined chapter. There's no truly good reason why English should be placed on a linguistic pedestal there, but that's where it sits, as much a part of the education system as history or math. Accordingly, the ideologies attached to the language – *including those regarding race* – have traveled overseas with our influence, and despite how distant they otherwise are from the United States or Canada, the hierarchies reminded me distinctly of home while I lived there.

In something of a sad way, **Algeria** is an example of a country whose relatively improved status in terms of modernity and liberation from explicit colonialism has resulted in their repeating the structures of those who had exerted control over them. They are hardly the only country that has learned from its former 'owners', but the status of sub-Saharan Africans as sub-Algerian is a reminder that just throwing off the shackles of colonialism doesn't mean you're free from its ideologies. And of course, as with any part of the 'MENA' region, we in the United States don't help by portraying an entire portion of the world as villainous, because, like Mexico, this especially hurts the people within the countries who need more support than they're receiving at home.

New England, as its name suggests, is one of the least diverse parts of the United States, while simultaneously being one of the richest and most educated. It very outwardly believes in its own unique value, but because it is mostly liberal politically, it feels even more moral superiority. It's the oldest part of the country, and is thus the reason the whole country exists as such, having thrown off the Crown once upon a time. Accordingly, it's hard to tell them they're wrong when they can point to the results as being objectively positive for their region. And yet it's no mystery for me, with as much time as I've spent there, why people like me tend to stay away.

Finland is often ranked as the best country, the happiest country, the smartest country, all those sorts of things. And, whether or not that data is precisely accurate, this international praise prevents internal honesty about issues that persist. There are obviously lessons to be learned from certain things that are done well in Finland, things I wish we did in the United States, but what incentive is there to challenge oneself if you're already at or near the top?

I used **Italy** as a sort of proxy for a group whose status has greatly changed within the United States, from their beginnings as disrespected and barely above newly freed slaves, to the way our public pedagogy valorized a certain version of their customs, to the present day, when they are firmly classified as white in the United States, but hold onto their justifiable wounds from the not-too-distant past. Yet within the country itself, there are plenty of people who would tell you just how hard it is to be seen as an actual Italian if you don't look the right way.

And finally, like many of the places in this book, I as a lifelong resident of the **New York City** area was unwilling or unable to look honestly at my home until far too late. We are indeed diverse and we are indeed full of different cultures, but when there is conflict, we are no more immune to turning on the most vulnerable among us, people usually so positioned because of class, race and language, and it simply makes me very sad to have to admit this now.

So Where Do We Go from Here?

I have three pieces of advice based on what I've learned, and what it was like to try and put these stories together. These are technically advice for each place, country or context mentioned, but countries don't read, people do, so ultimately it's meant to be taken and performed by the individuals consuming my work. Essentially, what can YOU do if you're a member of one of the places in question, or even if you're not and just want to help challenge and change the story?

But ultimately, this isn't truly about what we should do. This is really about what we need to not do. To that end …

1. Don't Dismiss

This is easier said than done, but when you find out something unpleasant about your home or the place where you live, it's natural to feel discomfort and perhaps a bit of cognitive dissonance. Especially if you are a member of majoritized groups – *and we almost all are in some way given our access to education and such* – then you are likely to find yourself in a situation where you've been comforted and supported and welcomed while others haven't. It can be unmooring to feel that your stability is happenstance or illusory.

Additionally, even if you nominally care about oppressed groups, if you are in the position that many of us are, in a privileged class position but minoritized racially or linguistically or something similar, there's always the temptation to rest on your specific lack of power. You're aware that this oppression is harmful, even directly to you, but we might feel it's not necessary to plumb deeper into our homes and resist the stories being told around, and about, us. Yet I think it's clear by now that, since we spend the first few decades of our lives being batted around by these narratives, we all have a part to play in crafting a new one.

In the Pacific Northwest, for example, when you hear people praise the progressivism of the area and feel pride accordingly, consider challenging this story with a meta-conversation about said progressive perception. This is the region of some legitimately awe-inspiring work, but it's also the place where people crowd out minoritized voices. Especially if you are in a position of relative power, take a step back and consider how you can avoid falling into this pattern, and don't dismiss the fact that you are just as fallible as everyone else who's come before you.

I can imagine that if you live in a place where the specific racial hierarchy of anti-Blackness feels distant, some of these revelations are easy to set aside, as might be the case in South Korea or Japan. I even told myself that when people pointed at me in awe it was because I wasn't Korean, not specifically because I was Black, and while there's some truth to that, raciolinguistic ideologies and their associated harms are in fact Occam's Razor most of the time, so instead of twisting ourselves into avoiding the possibility that the story is globally prevalent, we should, nay must, sit with what this means. And we have to keep sitting with it, forever.

It's hard to get over this hump or kneejerk dismissal, though. It's simply inconvenient to understand you've benefited from a cultural myopia or collective dishonesty, and because the causes are so diffuse, it's difficult to point a finger effectively. Indeed, the frothing anger that conservatives around the globe feel when asked to simply sit with the past is evidence that this is not an easy thing to do. After however many years of therapy, I understand how much more comfortable it is to get angry and dismiss an uncomfortable truth than to just exist within it, so I'm hardly immune to these human foibles. Indeed, as I'll explain in the next section, despite how dangerous their behavior is, I actually understand why they're so mad, as this is a heavy cognitive and emotional load that cannot be fully dislodged.

Let me give you a more specific example of dismissal and learning to move past this impulse.

A little more than 10 years ago, when the initial wave of Black Lives Matters protests occurred in 2014, I wasn't someone who talked very much about racism, and certainly not about raciolinguistic ideologies given its most prominent articles had yet to be published, though I'm sure Drs. Flores and Rosa were hard at work on the gifts they soon gave us. Those experiences I told you about in my NYC youth had occurred, but it would be years yet before I'd come to my current understanding of my city. No, at this point the aspect of racism I could no longer dismiss was more personal.

I had started running marathons by this point, and the good thing about running is that almost anyone can do it, which means you meet a lot of different types of people you would otherwise never have met. The bad thing about running is that almost anyone can do it, which means you meet a lot of different types of people you would have otherwise avoided. When those protests occurred, I was shocked to see people I knew calling them 'thugs' and 'animals', shocked not just by their racism but that they would use such language while well aware I would be able to see it. My first impulse was dismissiveness – they weren't keeping track of their 'friend' lists and didn't think too much that they had Black acquaintances. But that was avoiding the issue. My second impulse was to assume explicit malice, that they wanted me and others to see how they felt, but this is not actually grappling with the issue, and fits into the overarching master narrative that some small number of people are just Bad and Mean, and that that's where racism persists. No, the reality was more complex, and required deeper thought.

Ultimately, I realized that they were aware I was there, and thought I'd either agree with them or accept their commentary without challenging it. Unlike the current version of Twitter/X, this was still when people tried to be relatively civil within their Facebook friendships, and they thought I was *not that type of Black person*. I argued with them, deleted a few of them, and tried to move on. But what it helped me understand was that, though my Blackness is obvious, they were classifying me as One Of The Good Ones, who wouldn't ruffle their feathers. My response to this has been more than a decade of speaking out much more directly, assessing how much I can trust friends – *especially, but hardly exclusively, the white ones* – on these issues, and sitting with how I'd reached 28 without people believing I was not going to be disturbed by their behavior. I'd already had my narrative changed on the United States, I was yet to have my narrative changed on NYC, but I could no longer dismiss the information I was being given on the narrative that existed about me and the way I moved through the world. And refusing to dismiss that was one of the best and most productive decisions I've ever made, even though it made me horribly sad at the beginning. Indeed, a lot of this work is emotional, and to, again, dismiss the internal impact of these actions would be silly of me. These hierarchies cause material harm but emotional devastation as well, so of course trying to change the story would stir up strong feelings all the same. No one said it would be easy, but I still contend it's worth the effort.

So when you're confronted with truths about the untruths you've been taught, even if they make it hard to maintain the same level of affection for the environment in which you've been raised or the culture you're most connected to, don't dismiss that discomfort. Look into it, read about it, write about it, talk about it and work on it. There is no other way.

2. Don't Lecture

It's tempting, especially if you are an educator or an academic of some sort, to believe that your relatively large body of knowledge requires you to inform everyone around you of what they don't yet know. And ultimately, this belief is supported by the fact that, admittedly, you're right, in terms of your efforts to push against these ideologies. You are indeed on the right side of facts, oppression, history, whatever you want to call it. There are so many people who are so deeply invested in perpetuating harmful structures that merely resisting this should render all of our efforts righteous. Yet there's a difference between being right and righteous, and being effective in effecting change.

I don't want anyone to get this twisted: I am by no means saying we should moderate or dilute our views to make incremental progress. No, I am instead warning against the way that adults react to the perception that they lack understanding and knowledge when they haven't, say, signed up for a degree-granting program. It's not okay to treat children as empty vessels, but for better or worse, they have little choice about their education. With adults, though, and I say this with more than a decade of experience guiding and teaching adult learners, if they think you think they're incompetent, they're just never going to listen to a thing you say. In fact, they might just run in the opposite direction ideologically to make a silly point.

Once again, I'm not any better than anyone I'm describing. In the run-up to the 2016 American Presidential election, I didn't know much about Bernie Sanders. During some early debate between Senator Sanders and Hillary Clinton, I was at a bar for a watch party, and he said something that I can't for the life of me remember, but it was exciting yet I was skeptical he could pull it off. I asked a nearby viewer about the mechanisms for achieving said goal, and I was immediately yelled at by a handful of people. Notably, all of these people were white.

Here in 2025 as I write this, I fully agree with what Sanders wanted to try and do. But in that moment, since no one was willing to engage with my question without dismissing its validity, I spent the rest of the primary wanting him to lose (and he did). That's petty! But people are petty. So if confronted with a counternarrative about a country's reality with regard to race and language, you cannot assume that simply providing the facts will win the day. Everyone, even the people who care enough about this to read this book – *or write it* – has their own journey into reality. I think it's vital that we hold two assumptions in our head at the same time: that everyone is fully capable of re-learning the story of the context that surrounds them; and that everyone could always stand to learn more. By placing these two ideas alongside each other, we can no longer scoff at someone's lack of understanding, because it just means they're not as far along in their journey as they may soon be. At the same time, it means that we have to assume people are acting in good faith, and are free to walk away from the effort when someone refuses to engage.

I truly think this is a massive societal problem, particularly among people I otherwise agree with politically. Maybe we've all forgotten that we had to learn not to follow these master narratives, but this is the water we all swim in, and it takes time, effort and happenstance to be pulled out to the shore. Indeed, I believe it might be the only way we can escape from these stories and their gravitational pull. We need to learn, and not dismiss what we come across, and then we understandably feel the desire to teach, but we absolutely have to believe in everyone's ability to make the same journey that we did.

I'm not asking anyone to forgive someone who brought harm to them or something like that. I am referring only to people who express a seemingly genuine desire to learn and grow. We need to be patient with people who are in the position we all once experienced, a collapse of their comfortable view of the world and an uncertain ideological future. The reason I encouraged all of us not to dismiss these hard truths is because having felt the urge to do so, we are thus better equipped to understand why others will struggle with the same changes.

The entire world is essentially throwing a public tantrum about being lectured on race, gender and other issues of equity and oppression. The bigotry and hierarchies were no more or less present before the past decade, but, especially after 2020, the world was inundated with well-meaning individuals who were ... kind of bad at teaching. The work that was produced was either so basic that it was difficult to progress beyond the master narrative, or so poorly communicated that it was impossible to learn from. Academia chose, as it always does, the esoteric, inaccessible approach, leaving the public to learn from people with less expertise and skill. I honestly think that, although a backlash to the moment of racial progress was inevitable, the depth and success of said backlash was only made possible by our complete failure to teach our fellow citizens effectively, to treat them as if they were fully capable of growth while admitting we ourselves were equally fallible and not to imply we believed we were superior to them for reaching a particular level of understanding earlier than they had.

I admit that I tend to get fairly worked up about this aspect of what I feel to be our possible paths to progress. I truly believe, as someone who has by now spent half his life teaching, that strong pedagogy is one of the rarest and most powerful things on the planet. At the same time, I think that bad teaching is incredibly harmful and destructive, but unless you've actually been trained in education – *and trained in a version of it that doesn't uphold that very same master narrative, which is exceedingly rare to find* – you really don't know what's what, the same way I don't know what good medical practices are. I say all this to say, this is why just being right isn't enough, because if you are perceived as condescending, your accuracy will not matter in the face of your audience's rejection of your approach.

You may be reading this thinking I've gone far afield from the book's subject, and, hey, I've been known to do that, but I don't actually believe that's the case here. The book is about a lot of different countries and regions, and about race and language and how they intersect, but it's really about the stories we tell ourselves about where we come from, and the stories we promote to the world about our cultures and countries. People rely heavily on quantitative data, but it's stories that stick with us, stories that guide us, for better or worse, and it's stories that help us teach most effectively. Unfortunately, the most effective and impactful story we've all been told is the one we only belatedly realize is already happening all around us.

But all is not hopeless, because my final piece of guidance is …

3. Don't Give Up

It can seem bleak out there. Will we all be trying to find high ground to even read books in 80 years once we live inside of *Waterworld*? Or will the next pandemic take us all out once our petulant response to (poorly communicated) public health guidance leaves us more vulnerable? Or maybe we'll finally just press the button and (the lightly fictionalized version of) *Oppenheimer* will be right that the world's already been destroyed. But if that's the case, there's probably not much you can do about it.

By which I do not mean you should be hopeless or nihilistic. Far from it. You shouldn't be myopic about the real problems we all face, you shouldn't dismiss issues you see, as I've already said. But giving up only helps the status quo persist. That's precisely what they want.

The final story I can tell you about all this is one where I'm not even diving into my memories but talking about people I've never met.

If you look at old versions of the United States census, they would list names, genders (or, sex, really), races and professions, among other things. A lot of these records are available for free online via various state depositories, so places such as Ancestry.com will let you look up your family tree to a certain extent (before you have to pay them). You can even use those sites to find relatives, and frankly I trust that far more than giving out my DNA to the shadier companies I'd rather stay away from.

Anyway, a while ago, when I was finishing up my doctorate, I got to wondering about my ancestors. I'd done this sort of research once before but hadn't gone very far back into the past, and this time I wanted to go as far as the trail would let me before it petered out. I found out some fun things, like confirming more definitively that I do have a Native American ancestor. A lot of Black families will say that, and I had believed it when I was young because why wouldn't I, but with all the scandals of people claiming ancestry they didn't have, I didn't ever really say it aloud because, aside from not actually knowing anything about that part of myself, I didn't have proof or tribal membership, though that would be interesting to pursue someday. I also found out I have an ancestor from Ireland who emigrated to Pennsylvania – *where my mother's family is from* – in the 19th century, and it turns out he owned a pub, which is a little funny. And yes, this does mean I'm some small percentage white.

On my dad's side, though, where my last name comes from, the line goes straight to North and South Carolina. My father was born in the former, and then every census said the same basic region going all the way back until the line gets fuzzy, and until it was clear said ancestors were not free citizens. And yes, as a call back to an earlier chapter, this was after the UK likes to claim it abolished slavery, so, bully for them.

Anyway, the line stops in a town called Galivants Ferry, South Carolina, in Horry County. There doesn't appear to be much of anything there. Shooting/rifle ranges, and farms, mostly. Speaking of the latter, though, there is one, short street called 'Gerald Farm Road'. Now. I have not gone all the way down there to personally investigate this, and the supposed Gerald Farm itself no longer seems to exist, nor do any actual Geralds seem to still live there, but given that Gerald is a last name (or surname) of British origin, and the timeframe I'm referring to, let's just say I'm pretty sure we didn't exactly own the farm, and that there was another type of ownership going on.

The first Geralds I could find listed on the census, all the adult males were described the same way. 'Negro', obviously, and, 'illiterate laborer'. This didn't change for decades. 'Illiterate laborer'. It's possible some of them could read or write in a basic way and the census takers were dismissing their skills, but I think you get the point.

One-hundred-eighty-ish years seems like a long time because it's much longer than a human lifespan, but in the grand scheme of human existence, it's a mere blip, let alone the overall evolution of ape-like creatures. My point is, there's no reason to believe that there was a sudden acceleration around the time of my grandparents' birth that allowed them to be particularly more capable than the Geralds that came before them. These illiterate laborers, who may have been confined to that farm in South Carolina, are very similar to me, yet I'm about as far an illiterate laborer as possible, not just because I have a doctorate and am an author, but also because I am pretty terrible at manual labor. However, I'm sure if it was all I had the opportunity to do, I'd be better than I am.

Anyway. What's my point? Indeed, what's the point of the whole book?

I come from people who could have given up. Could have seen their circumstances and decided to stop trying, knowing that they might have to watch their own children live in bondage just as they had. Any time someone tries to tell me that anything happening now is worse than it's ever been, it's clear that there's a lack of perspective, but I still have to resist that urge to lecture them, because even I hadn't sat down to think of this very concretely until a few years ago.

I encourage everyone reading this to think about how much our very existence depends on people who didn't give up. I encourage everyone reading this to believe me when I say that, although I do not by any means take *myself* all that seriously – *or else there wouldn't be an italicized joke in every other paragraph* – I absolutely take this work seriously, and we all should, because it's all of our collective responsibility to do so. It doesn't particularly matter what we see on the news, on social media or among our ongoing public pedagogy. What matters is that we take a step back to think about the stories we've been told, and start telling a different one.

Racism and harmful linguistic ideologies are everywhere. It's the same and different at the same time. It is absolutely not confined to the American South, or even to countries that are populated with white and Black people, or that speak English or other colonial languages. It's a big, ugly, mess of a concept, and it's not going anywhere any time soon. My sons will have to deal with it, and whichever Geralds come after them will have to do the same.

With all of that said, though, stories matter. Stories are passed down for decades, centuries, even millenia, and while it may well take us further millenia to create a wholly new master narrative about who is and isn't valuable and why, there's no reason you and I can't start re-writing our collective story today.

Epilogue

You know, it's funny to end this book talking about people who were forced to live in the American South when the whole impetus for writing it was to dispel the notion that that specific aspect of racism is not how these hierarchies work around the world, but that's the way the story worked out.

However, I did want to address something that may or may not be relevant given, if you're reading the epilogue, you presumably finished the whole book and found it compelling enough to keep going.

It was pointed out to me by one of the reviewers that it was possible no one would be interested in a book like this, which spends considerably more time wagging its finger at liberals and progressives than at conservatives that spew slurs. I conducted the interviews in late 2023, had to go off and write my second book in early 2024, became a father again literally on election day in November 2024 – *my older son was born right before the original COVID lockdown so these kids are harbingers of doom* – and then sat down to write this book just after that. I got the initial comments back in May of 2025 and am writing these words in June. By the time you are reading this in, at the earliest, February of 2026, maybe everyone who speaks the word 'Black' aloud will be in prison, so why would we care about the points I am making and not the direct, imminent threat in front of us?

Well.

First of all, you can go to any bookstore or airport right now and get 65 books about These Current Times that will probably tell you not very much you don't already know, or fart out rampant speculation that confirms your biases, like when I found a book in 2007 called, *Condi Vs. Hillary: The Next Great Presidential Race*. I am not making this up, you can find it in Bezos-land, but I'm not citing those authors for their immediately irrelevant nonsense. The point I'm making here is that I think, especially at Times Like These, it's important to think long-term about, in a sense, how we got here.

If you remember the brief promise of 2020 and the global anti-racist protests, there sure were a lot of people talking, but I do think that what I mentioned in the conclusion, about lecturing and giving up, helped us fall all the way back down the cliff. A lot of the people who grabbed the microphone were pretty bad spokespeople, and a lot of folks who were new to caring about marginalized groups lost patience with the fact that these ideologies are so entrenched and intransigent.

I wrote this to try and put forth the argument that this is a centuries-long fight we're in. It took them centuries to build these master narratives, yet they know the narratives are empty and transparent, so they have to expend energy on propping them up with various harmful policies. It's not going to be over anytime soon, not while I'm alive, and probably not even while my sons are, but if we can start to tell a different story, then, on whatever ice-cap-less version of the planet we're living on in the future, maybe we can come slightly closer to telling the truth.

Acknowledgments

So all of my books – *wow, what a wild thing to be able to say, 'books' plural* – have more or less the same list of acknowledgments. And since I've written three in four years, the people I've worked with and leaned on haven't changed very much.

As ever, I thank Anna Roderick and the staff at Multilingual Matters, and the reviewers who helped bring this book into the shape it has eventually reached. Unlike many people, I love to be edited if it's by someone who understands my vision, and they've always been great partners to work with.

I thank all of the teachers I've ever had who supported me, up to and including in my doctoral program, especially Dr. Catherine Voulgarides and Dr. Marshall George, who never scoffed at my writerly ambitions.

I also need to thank every teacher who *didn't* support me, as a Black boy with undiagnosed ADHD, because it has helped me always be considerate of those students or readers who've never been given correct guidance, and how I can best connect with them and their needs. I don't want to imply that being mistreated is a good thing in a 'what doesn't kill you makes you stronger' way, but the fact is, I learned what not to do as an educator from them, and I think about them all the time when I do my work with the students in front of me.

I obviously have to thank everyone who agreed to participate in these interviews, some of whom were already my friends or colleagues, and others whom I have since become close to. You may or may not realize it because I'm the one who wrote the book, but whenever I tell people about this project and they are excited, I know that it's only because of your contributions that this is possible.

To the professional organizations that have continued to hire me to speak and present and write, to the academic peers who continue to ask me to contribute to their issues and volumes, I appreciate your commitment to valuing my thinking and writing. I'm not even a full-time academic, I honestly do this because I enjoy it and because I think it matters, and yet it wouldn't be possible if I didn't continue to receive respect from the people who consume what I've produced.

My family remains steadfast in their support of me. My parents (including step- and -in-law), as well as my sister, my wife's siblings and all the nieces and nephews that are starting to become aware of the nonsense I engage in, no one has tried to slow my roll, and that matters a great deal.

My dog, Neptune, will continue to be thanked in these books until he's not around anymore, and though he has a funky way of showing it, his love for me and all of us is probably the least complex of anyone I spend time with. So long as he's been fed, all he wants is to be around me, and I shouldn't take that for granted, because he won't always be there to do so.

My wife knows how important all this writing is to me. She once said, in an exercise we were doing, that if I were ever to get famous it would be from my writing. This, as I've said, isn't my main job and isn't anything close to my primary source of income, but I wouldn't be whole without the work, so her support is invaluable and always will be.

My older son, Ezel, is going to be forced to read all my nonsense someday, and he's only got a few more years before all that starts. But as a person who somehow looks exactly like I did at his age, and who shares many of my personality quirks and characteristics, he has been a litmus test for my value ever since he was born back before the COVID lockdowns. Without him, I wouldn't have felt the need to get myself evaluated for ADHD, without him, I wouldn't have designed a course about race in the summer of 2020 that eventually turned into my dissertation – *and therefore allowed me to graduate as quickly as I did* – and without him, a lot of my first few efforts to make an impact just wouldn't have mattered. I owe him more than he'll ever understand.

But unlike the first two books, this time, there's another person I need to acknowledge, my younger son, Idris. He's all of one year old at the time of this book's release, so we can't even have real conversations yet, but if Ezel is any indication, he's going to be yet another reason I need to keep doing this work. I said in the conclusion that I damn well better not give up, despite the times that depressive thoughts try to convince me otherwise, and while Ezel is starting to understand the arc of race and Black history, Idris isn't there yet, and that's fine. I'm going to keep at this until there's no ideas left inside of me, because the Geralds from Galivants Ferry did that for me, and they didn't even know one of their descendants would someday be about as far from 'illiterate laborer' as possible.

And finally, as ever, I thank you for reading all of this. Writing a book that no one reads is pointless, so everyone who made it this far deserves my deep appreciation and care.

Now go change that story you've been told. The best time to have done this was years ago, but the second best time is always now.

Dr. Justin Pierce Baldwin Gerald

Citations!

Allen, R. (2023) Get out: Structural racism and academic terror (April 23, 2022). *William & Mary Journal of Women and the Law* 29 (3), 2023. St. John's Legal Studies Research Paper No. 22-0003. Available at SSRN: https://ssrn.com/abstract=4091637

Arab Barometer (2019) Survey data analysis tool. See https://www.arabbarometer.org/survey-data/data-analysis-tool/

Arellano, A. (2022) American expats in Mexico: A controversy. *Los Angeles Times*, 29 July. See https://www.latimes.com/california/story/2022-07-29/american-expats-mexico-controversy

Benrabah, M. (2005) The language planning situation in Algeria. *Current Issues in Language Planning* 6 (4), 379–502. https://doi.org/10.1080/14664208.2005.10807312

Blaec, C. (2020) The complicated rise and swift fall of Portland's Wall of Moms protest group. *Portland Monthly*, 5 August. See https://www.pdxmonthly.com/news-and-city-life/2020/08/the-complicated-rise-and-swift-fall-of-portland-s-wall-of-moms-protest-group

Block, S. (2019) Grenfell Tower inquiry: Building regulations. *Dezeen*, 1 November. See https://www.dezeen.com/2019/11/01/grenfell-tower-inquiry-building-regulations/

Bonilla-Silva, E. (2017) *Racism without Racists: Color-Blind Racism and the Persistence of Racial Inequality in America* (5th edn). Rowman & Littlefield.

Cann, C.N. (2013) What school movies and TFA teach us about who should teach urban youth: Dominant narratives as public pedagogy. *Urban Education* 50 (3), 288–315. https://doi.org/10.1177/0042085913507458 (Original work published 2015).

Census (2024) See https://furmancenter.org/neighborhoods/view/jamaica-hollis

Center for Democratic Renewal (n.d.) Racist and far right organizing in the Pacific Northwest (NCJ No. 122261). National Institute of Justice. See https://www.ojp.gov/ncjrs/virtual-library/abstracts/racist-and-far-right-organizing-pacific-northwest

Chan, S. (2007) The Abner Louima case: 10 years later. *The New York Times*, 9 August. See https://archive.nytimes.com/cityroom.blogs.nytimes.com/2007/08/09/the-abner-louima-case-10-years-later/

Charles, Q. (2019) Black teachers of English in South Korea: Constructing identities as a native English speaker and English language teaching professional. *TESOL Journal* 10 (4), 1–19.

Clean Clothes Campaign (2020) Forced labour and debt trap: Migrant workers in Japan face substantial risks during coronavirus outbreak. See https://cleanclothes.org/news/2020/forced-labour-and-debt-trap-migrant-workers-in-japan-face-substantial-risks-during-coronavirus-outbreak-

Cornell Law School (2024) Redlining. See https://www.law.cornell.edu/wex/redlining#:~:text=Redlining%20can%20be%20defined%20as,on%20their%20race%20or%20ethnicity

Cornell Legal Information Institute (2024) See https://www.law.cornell.edu/wex/redlining

Creative Spirits (2024) Stereotypes & prejudice of 'Aboriginal Australia'. See https://www.creativespirits.info/aboriginalculture/people/stereotypes-prejudice-of-aboriginal-australia#good-stereotypes-australias-tourism-industry

Durand-Moreau, Q., Lafontaine, J. and Ward, J. (2022) See https://pubmed.ncbi.nlm.nih.gov/35839817/

Dunbar-Ortiz, R. (2014) *An Indigenous Peoples' History of the United States*. Beacon Press.

European Commission (2024) Organisation of private education in Finland. See https://eurydice.eacea.ec.europa.eu/national-education-systems/finland/organisation-private-education#:~:text=In%20Finland%20most%20private%20schools,of%20the%20level%20of%20education

Fanon, F. (1952) *Black Skin, White Masks*. C. L. Markmann (trans). Grove Press.

Fekete, L. (2004) Anti-Muslim racism and the European security state. *Race & Class* 46 (1), 3–29.

Fletcher, M. (2023) Blind Side subject Michael Oher alleges adoption was a lie; family took all film proceeds. *ESPN*, 8 September. See https://www.espn.com/nfl/story/_/id/38190720/blind-side-subject-michael-oher-alleges-adoption-was-lie-family-took-all-film-proceeds

Garcia, N. (2021) Orange Shirt Day: Uncovering the dark history of residential schools in Canada. *Cultural Survival*. See https://www.culturalsurvival.org/news/orange-shirt-day-uncovering-dark-history-residential-schools-canada

Gerald, J.P.B. (2020) Worth the risk: Towards decentring whiteness in English language teaching. *BC TEAL Journal* 5 (1), 44–54. https://doi.org/10.14288/bctj.v5i1.345

Gerald, J.P.B. (2022a) *Antisocial Language Teaching: English and the Pervasive Pathology of Whiteness*. Multilingual Matters. https://doi.org/10.21832/9781800413283

Gerald, J.P.B. (2022b) The 'Ezel Project' inquiry: Mesotransformative praxis to decenter whiteness in racialized organizations and schools [Dissertation, CUNY Academic Works]. See https://academicworks.cuny.edu/hc_sas_etds/892

Gonzalez-Sobrino, B. and Goss, D.R. (2019) Exploring the mechanisms of racialization beyond the black–white binary. *Ethnic and Racial Studies* 42 (4), 505–510. https://doi.org/10.1080/01419870.2018.1444781

Guinness World Records (2024) Most countries to have gained independence from the same country. Guinness World Records. See https://www.guinnessworldrecords.com/world-records/most-countries-to-have-gained-independence-from-the-same-country

Hammack, P.L. and Toolis, E.E. (2015) Putting the social into personal identity: The master narrative as root metaphor for psychological and developmental science. *Human Development* 58 (6), 350–364.

Hassanein, A. (2024, April 19) Census change will lead to more data on health of Middle Eastern North African people in the U.S. *Stateline*, 19 April. See https://stateline.org/2024/04/19/census-change-will-lead-to-more-data-on-health-of-middle-eastern-north-african-people-in-us/#:~:text=For%20decades%2C%20U.S.%20residents%20with,housing%20and%20other%20important%20markers

Himmelstein, M. (2021) Why white children and communities need diverse books and libraries. *School Library Journal*. See https://www.slj.com/story/why-white-children-and-communities-need-diverse-books-libraries-antiracism

Hoegaerts, J., Peterson, E., Liimatainen, T. and Hekanaho, L. (2022) Finnishness, whiteness and coloniality: An introduction. In J. Hoegaerts, T. Liimatainen, L. Hekanaho and E. Peterson (eds) *Finnishness, Whiteness and Coloniality* (pp. 1–16). Helsinki University Press. https://doi.org/10.33134/HUP-17-1

Hulme, P. and Youngs, T. (eds) (2002) *The Cambridge Companion to Travel Writing*. Cambridge University Press. https://doi.org/10.1017/CCOL052178140X

Ignatiev, N. (1995) *How the Irish became White*. Routledge.

Jim Crow Museum, Ferris State University (2023) See https://jimcrowmuseum.ferris.edu/question/2023/september23.htm

Kim, M., Choi, D. and Kim, T. (2019a) South Korean jobseekers' perceptions and (de)motivation to study for standardized English tests in neoliberal corporate labor markets. *The Asian EFL Journal* 21 (1), 84–109.

Kim, R., Roberson, L., Russo, M. and Briganti, P. (2019b) Language diversity, nonnative accents, and their consequences at the workplace: Recommendations for individuals, teams, and organizations. *The Journal of Applied Behavioral Science* 55, 73–95.

Know Your Meme (2024) Are we the baddies? See https://knowyourmeme.com/memes/are-we-the-baddies

Livingston, C. (2021) Ted Cruz goes to Cancun during power outage. *Texas Tribune*, 18 February. See https://www.texastribune.org/2021/02/18/ted-cruz-cancun-power-outage/

Maghbouleh, N. (2017) *The Limits of Whiteness: Iranian Americans and the Everyday Politics of Race*. Stanford University Press.

Maghbouleh, N., Schachter, A. and Flores, R.D. (2022) Middle Eastern and North African Americans may not be perceived, nor perceive themselves, to be white. *Proceedings of the National Academy of Sciences of the United States of America* 119 (7), e2117940119. https://doi.org/10.1073/pnas.2117940119

Mater, J. (2022) Troubled teen industry: Its effects. *Inquiry Journal*, April. See https://www.unh.edu/inquiryjournal/blog/2022/04/troubled-teen-industry-its-effects-oral-history

Mexican Census (2020) See https://www.inegi.org.mx/contenidos/programas/ccpv/2020/doc/Censo2020_Principales_resultados_EUM.pdf

Mexico City Tourism Board (2024) Getting around in Mexico City. See https://mexicocity.cdmx.gob.mx/e/getting-around/

Migration Policy Institute (2024) Australia. See https://www.migrationpolicy.org/country-resource/australia

Mills, C. and Lefrancois, B. (2018) Child as metaphor: Colonialism, psygovernance, and epistemicide. *World Futures* 74 (7–8), 503–524.

MyLifeElsewhere (n.d.) France vs. Texas size comparison. See https://www.mylifeelsewhere.com/country-size-comparison/france/texas-usa

National Center on Education and the Economy (2021) Finland: Demographic and economic data. See https://documents.ncsl.org/wwwncsl/Education/Study-Group/2.FinlandDemoEconDataNCEE.pdf

National Library of Australia (2024) Convicts. See https://www.nla.gov.au/research-guides/convicts

National Museum of Australia (2024) White Australia policy. See https://www.nma.gov.au/defining-moments/resources/white-australia-policy#:~:text=On%2023%20December%201901%20the,non%2DBritish%20migration%20to%20Australia

Navarre (2024) See https://www.usnews.com/news/best-countries/articles/2024-03-20/why-finland-is-the-worlds-happiest-country

New Hampshire Public Radio (2021) Invisible walls: Many refugees are funneled into a few Manchester neighborhoods. See https://www.nhpr.org/nh-news/2022-04-01/invisible-walls-many-refugees-are-funneled-into-a-few-manchester-neighborhoods

Office of National Statistics (2024) See https://www.ons.gov.uk/peoplepopulationandcommunity/populationandmigration/populationestimates

Olosuga, K. (2015) British history of slavery buried at scale revealed. *The Guardian*, 12 July. See https://www.theguardian.com/world/2015/jul/12/british-history-slavery-buried-scale-revealed

Omi, M. and Winant, H. (2014) *Racial Formation in the United States* (3rd edn). Routledge. https://doi.org/10.4324/9780203076804

Oregon Remembrance Project (2023) The history of racial exclusion in Oregon. See https://oregonremembrance.org/sunrise-project/the-history/#:~:text=Racial%20Exclusion%20in%20Oregon&text=However%2C%20by%201930%2C%2028%20of,was%20once%20a%20sundown%20town (accessed 23 October 2023).
Painter, N.I. (2011) *The History of White People*. W.W. Norton.
Ramos, C. (2024) South Korea accused of abuse with seasonal worker scheme. *Context News*. See https://www.context.news/socioeconomic-inclusion/south-korea-accused-of-abuse-with-seasonal-worker-scheme
Rawlinson, K. (2018) Windrush: 11 people wrongly deported from UK have died, Sajid Javid. *The Guardian*, 12 November. See https://www.theguardian.com/uk-news/2018/nov/12/windrush-11-people-wrongly-deported-from-uk-have-died-sajid-javid
Ricento, T. (2013) The consequences of official bilingualism on the status and perception of non-official languages in Canada. *Journal of Multilingual and Multicultural Development* 34 (5), 475–489. https://doi.org/10.1080/01434632.2013.783034
Ripley, A. (2013) *The Smartest Kids in the World: And How They Got that Way*. Simon & Schuster.
Robinson, C.J. (1983) *Black Marxism: The Making of the Black Radical Tradition*. Zed Books.
Ruecker, T. and Ives, L. (2015) White native English speakers needed: The rhetorical construction of privilege in online teacher recruitment spaces. *TESOL Quarterly* 49 (4), 733–754.
Sander (2020) See https://www.midstory.org/the-politics-of-midwestern-identity-racial-divides/
Soguel, D. (2022) They are Black. They are Italians. And they are changing their country. *Christian Science Monitor*, 26 September. See https://www.csmonitor.com/World/Europe/2022/0926/They-are-Black.-They-are-Italians.-And-they-are-changing-their-country
Staples, B. (2019) How Italians became 'white'. *The New York Times*, 12 October. See https://www.nytimes.com/interactive/2019/10/12/opinion/columbus-day-italian-american-racism.html
Statistics Canada (2022) The Canadian census: A rich portrait of the country's religious and ethnocultural diversity, 26 October. https://www150.statcan.gc.ca/n1/daily-quotidien/
UK Government (2021) See https://www.gov.uk/government/publications/the-report-of-the-commission-on-race-and-ethnic-disparities
US Census (2020) See https://worldpopulationreview.com/states/by-race
US Census (2022) See https://statisticalatlas.com/division/New-England/Educational-Attainment
US Census (2023) See https://worldpopulationreview.com/states/california; https://census-reporter.org/profiles/03000US1-new-england-division/
US Census (2024) See https://worldpopulationreview.com/us-cities/new-york/yonkers
US Dept of Commerce (2024) See https://datausa.io/profile/geo/united-states
Will (2020) See https://www.pewresearch.org/short-reads/2024/09/24/key-facts-about-public-school-teachers-in-the-u-s/
Williams, J.C. (2017) *White Working Class: Overcoming Class Cluelessness in America*. Harvard Business Review Press.
World Population Review (2023) See https://worldpopulationreview.com/states/washington
World Population Review (2025) See https://worldpopulationreview.com/countries/canada
Zamudio, M. M., and Rios, F. (2006) From traditional to liberal racism: Living racism in the everyday. *Sociological Perspectives* 49 (4), 483–501. https://doi.org/10.1525/sop.2006.49.4.483 (Original work published 2006).
Zoellner (2020) See https://www.independent.co.uk/news/world/americas/portland-wall-of-moms-protest-federal-officers-trump-a9635066.html

Index

The ones that are italicized are pop culture references, the ones that aren't are news stories or theory/concepts

Abner Louima, 115
ADHD, vii, viii, 1, 133, 134
Anchorman, 55

Black Lives Matter, 16, 35, 110, 123

Color-evasiveness, 48, 49, 76

Fargo, 8

Gangnam Style, 75, 78
Gangs of New York, 106
Get Out, 89, 90, 93
Green Book, 15
Green Room, 15
Grenfell, 36

Hollywood, 47, 50, 56

Know Your Meme, 37

Lonely Planet, 34, 35

Master narrative, 12, 17, 41, 42, 57, 61, 62, 84, 86, 99, 104, 105, 107, 108, 111, 112, 115, 117, 124, 125, 126, 129, 132

Native speakerism, 72, 73

Oppenheimer, 127

Portlandia, 5
Public pedagogy (note I excluded the title and the running title from this), 50, 52, 54, 64, 78, 88, 89, 111, 115, 120, 121, 129

Residential schools, 24, 25, 27, 119

Seinfeld, 114
Silicon Valley, 47, 48, 120
Sundown towns, 8, 15, 34, 55, 57, 58, 61, 89, 120

That Mitchell and Webb Look, 36
The Blind Side, 53, 54
The Godfather, 105, 106
The Knick, 106
Troubled teens, 50, 51,
Twilight, 16

Wall of Moms, 16-17
Waterworld, 127
West Side Story, 113
White Australia, 42, 43, 49
Windrush, 36

For Product Safety Concerns and Information please contact our EU Authorised Representative:

Easy Access System Europe

Mustamäe tee 50

10621 Tallinn

Estonia

gpsr.requests@easproject.com

www.ingramcontent.com/pod-product-compliance
Lightning Source LLC
Chambersburg PA
CBHW071438160426
43195CB00013B/1947